Graffiti Mural:
My Off the Wall Creative Writing

Eartha Watts Hicks

DEDICATION

To every family member who reveled in my uniqueness, reminded me that I was "special," and assured me that special was a good thing;

To every educator who has urged me to be creative;

To the indie author, Valerie Chandler-Smith, who knew my first manuscript was 500 pages sitting in a deep drawer and chided me to *set my art free*;

To every artist fighting daily to protect their vision and profit from their creative gift;

To all my (s)heroes of prose and verse, most especially the astounding Ms. Poetically Nikki;

And to the musical genius whose firm grasp on his own individuality dared the entire world to embrace him in his ruffles and lace...

My focus, this time, was not so much to ensure the art was free from error, but simply to set it free and let it breathe.

CONTENTS

ACKNOWLEDGMENTS

To God be the glory. This work was especially made possible by The Harlem Writers Guild, Project Enterprise, The Center for Black Literature at Medgar Evers College, The Hurston-Wright Foundation, Cultivating Our Sisterhood International Association, Future Executives, Incorporated, The Langston Hughes Community Library and Cultural Center, The New York City Housing Authority Branch of the NAACP, Union Grove Baptist Church, and most especially my pastor and members of Gustavus Adolphus Lutheran Church.

A monetary donation of any amount to any of these organizations would further assist in empowering others.

This work was also made possible through the assistance of Mr & Mrs. Aaron Hill, Mr. Daniel Tisdale and Harlem World Magazine, Ms. Simone Monet Wahls and Future Executives, Inc., Ms. Althea Burton, Ms. Winnie Burch, Ms. Karen Vanderburg, Ms. Janet Samuels, Ms. Portia Blake, Ms. Robin Martinez, Ms. Kelli Jonee Smith, Ms. Lois Reddick, my editors Ms. Femi Lewis and Ms. Tumika Patrice Cain, Mr. David L. Russell, Mr. Charles Watts, Ms. Gloria Watts-Garner, Mr. & Mrs. Kevin Adams, Mr.

George Streeter, Aunt Carole and the Badgett family (Teaira, Spike, Delilah, Alicia, Yolanda and Uncle Bob), Ms. Olympia Small, Mr. Kenneth Watts, Mr. Kevin Watts, Ms. Dolores Armstrong, Ms. Eve Robinson, Ms. Miriam Kelly Ferguson, Mr. Clinton Long, Ms. Chaundra Cynn Moore, Ms. Nicole Goodwin, Ms. Lynn Spivey, Ms. Paula Inga, Ms. Bernice Watson, Mr. George Williams of Open Choice IT, Ms. Miraque Hicks and the Kissing Pages Blogsite, Say Wha?? Book Club, Mr. Jeff Gatsby and the D.J. Gatsby Book Club, Ms. Leona Romich and the OOSA Book Club, Ms. Sharon Blount and the Building Relationships Around Books Book Club, Ms. Deborah Grant, Ms. Crystal McKay, Mr. Lawrence Ben Miles and the New York Women's Chamber of Commerce, Ms. Cassandra Williams and the ladies of COSIA.

Note: While I can take credit for the content, formatting and cover design, I must acknowledge and extend a formal thank you to Urban Manga & Graffiti Artist Rakim Villanueva, for the oh, so authentic and original, hand-sketched graffiti art logo. I must also give credit and thanks to photographer Kenny Graham of JDStarz Photography for the fierce cover photo, and also send a huge thank you to Mr. Navi Robins, for his oh-so-fierce-cover-design for Graffiti Mural 2.

PROSE

NO MORE GOODWIN, LIVINGS, & MOORE

Romell Goodwin is a young, aspiring, Wall Street executive. He is talented and overconfident, but despite his intelligence and incredible drive, opportunities elude him. No More Goodwin, Livings & Moore is the tale of how he comes to realize that workplace politics are never fair. **This selection was first published in LOVING BLACK MEN: An Anthology released from Castle Black Publishing, edited by Mel and Christopher Bynum.**

My last day at Livings & Moore began just like any other day. I walked into the office suite, and as usual, the first person I saw was leggy, Kathy Barker. Immediately left of the doorway, hers were bare and crossed at the knee. Bouncing her foot drew attention to her thighs. I acknowledged Kathy by nodding in her direction, but ignored her when she winked back. Coffee was already brewing. Dark roast was in the air. "Good morning, Mr. Goodwin. You're looking handsome as ever." Kathy's very high, open-toe shoes stepped from around the reception counter over to the Espresso machine. She started as a temp with three responsibilities: answer phones, make copies, and bring coffee. Her message taking was so bad, we automated the system, and everyone now resorted to making their own copies. It was definitely Kathy's breast job that transformed an office of men into caffeine addicts. The few times I had her coffee, there were grounds floating in it. It was like I was drinking dirt. Still, Kathy won herself a permanent position with benefits. As usual, her dress was a second skin. Judging by the length of it, she was looking for a raise.

"Good morning, Miss Barker. None for me today, but thanks." Somehow, I always knew she was setting a trap for someone. It wouldn't be this homeboy. Instinctively, I stayed away.

"I'm starting to feel unappreciated," she said.

I kept my head and my face straight when I answered, "Don't. Everyone else loves your coffee."

As I walked through the aisles, I passed newspapers, half-eaten bagels, and cups of Kathy's fuel. For the longest time, I was always here first. Somehow my work ethic had changed the dynamic. These days, half the firm was eager enough to show up more than an hour early. A leaning stack of reports was waiting on my desk. I walked up, took off my blazer, and hung it on the edge of my cubicle. Then, I laid my newspaper down and pulled my HP out of my briefcase. On top of the reports was a lone sheet of paper. I chucked it into the in-tray and sat. In this business, information is crucial. My mind was already in process mode. I grabbed one of those second-quarter reports and flipped through it.

Anyone who paid attention knew I was not one for small talk. But, there's always one. "Hey, Romell. What's happening? Those are some bad-ass shoes, my man."

That was Ian Sharpe. My loafers were Bruno Maglis. They were stylish, I'll give him that much. Had I been wearing goldfish platforms, an Afro, bell bottoms, and a Dashiki, maybe I would've slapped him five on the black-hand side and we both could've done the Boogaloo to Wild Cherry. But this was 1995 and this white boy was sounding like a pimp plucked from a blaxploitation flick. I knew these guys here considered me a threat, because I was young, only twenty-five years old, and hungry. I was the only brother in Livings & Moore to make it out of the mailroom, because I asked "too many questions" about our employee stock options. I have dark skin and the bald head. My height and athletic build would be considered physically imposing, were it not for the fact that I happen to be so incredibly good looking. Realizing I'm a presence, I'd come to work dressed better than most, first in Armani and now, custom tailored. Ian still felt it necessary to approach me with slick jive talk. I didn't teach (ESL) Ebonics as a Second Language. I was the senior analyst that trained him. We were the same age, but I had much more time vested with the company, because I completed undergrad in two and a half years. I lost all respect for the guy when I learned he was a mediocre ivy leaguer, whose daddy had the wherewithal to pull strings to get him in here, but thanks to me, Ian passed the exam. Now, he'd been licensed long enough to start figuring shit out on his own. Still he always seemed to find his way over to pester me when I had a ton of work to do, making every day a struggle not to punch him in the mouth.

When I didn't look up from my report, I guess he took it to mean I didn't hear him. He spoke louder. "Hey, my main man, I was searching through the firm's network, trying to locate that spreadsheet of yours, and I couldn't find it."

"You won't."

"Why not?"

"I developed those formulas. Those are my calculations. All my files are encrypted with a password and not backed up to the server. Any more questions?"

"How did you come up with something that complex?"

"I know what I'm doing."

"You must really have a high IQ."

"Nah, Ian. Mensa accepts retards. Now, if you don't mind," I pointed to the stack of the reports sitting on my desk and shooed him away with a hand gesture.

"Okay, just so you know. I picked you for my team. I'm sending an email with the details. I look forward to working together, man."

Ian left my cubicle just as Nick was walking by. Nick's a white boy, but his mother's Korean, and so is his wife for that matter. The first time I saw him, he seemed unusual and I couldn't pinpoint why. He's of average build and wore the standard blue suit, pale blue shirt, red tie, and Oxfords, just like every white boy in here. He's got the thick dark straight hair, darker skin, and eye shape that hinted at something. I found myself staring trying to figure out what that was, but I couldn't tell Nick was part Asian until I saw him standing with his wife. Nick was one of the coolest cats in the office, a pompous go-getter, but a straight shooter. Maybe, that's why we clicked. I smiled at Nick, shook my head, and said, "Good morning."

He walked over and sat, "You're taking this a lot better than I expected."

"Of course I am. I just roll with it. I don't let anything bother me," I said, but when I saw the shock in his expression, it occurred to me to ask, "What exactly do you mean?"

"Ian's promotion."

"Ian's promotion to what?"

He leaned in and whispered, "They're launching a major hedge fund. Ian was chosen to head up the technology division. That's the memo right there. Didn't you read it?"

I jumped up, and snatched the sheet out of my tray. Just like Nick said, it was announcing Ian's promotion. I paced for about a minute. Then, I marched over to Stevenson's office and knocked on his big mahogany door. When he said the word, I entered.

Stevenson looked up from his daily planner. The buttons on his blue dress shirt struggled to stay closed, while his undershirt played peek-a-boo. "What can I do for you, Romell?"

Standing in front of him, I said, "Mr. Stevenson, I have some concerns. I'd like to know exactly when I can expect my promotion."

"That's a little forward. Don't you think?"

"Maybe, but it seems to me this firm is handing out promotions like candy. If so, I'd like mine now."

"I take it you've read the memo."

I wanted to say: Fuck a memo! Somebody at this firm is purposely trying to fuck with me! But, I smiled and said, "Yes, Mr. Stevenson, sir. I've read the announcement. The fact that you guys gave away a position, that rightfully should have been mine, lets me know that no one here appreciates all the effort I'm putting in."

"That appointment was a decision of the board. It was not my doing. My advice to you is to just hang in there and try to make the best of it. In due time—"

"I've done my part!" I was extremely agitated, but I saw Stevenson reach for the intercom, probably to call security. I took a deep breath to calm myself and continued to object. "No. You're asking too much. I can't. I won't. In fact, I'd like to see how Ian's going to head up the tech division without my help."

"Why? Are you going somewhere?"

"Maybe. I have several offers." The truth was, I didn't want to work anywhere else. I was hoping I could move through the ranks here at Livings & Moore, until this place changed its name. Goodwin, Livings & Moore always did seem to have a nice ring to it.

Stevenson folded his hands and sat them on his gut. "Several offers, eh?"

"Big ones." Right then, I thought about my friend, Mia, and how she was trying to convince me to circulate my résumé and give the higher ups my list of demands and an ultimatum. Promote me or else. To me, all that was just tough talk from someone working for peanuts. I did not say what I said because I was following her advice. The money I was making was enough to appease me. I said what I said, because I had backed myself into a corner and didn't know what else to say. I knew I had a good head on my shoulders, and besides that, I was just plain tired of kissing up, smiling when I was pissed off, not being able to talk back, all so these assholes would one day throw me a bone. In a perfect world, I would already have contacted some head hunters or at the very least had a Plan B. I would've had something better lined up. In that perfect world, I would've told that fat bastard just how fat he was.

"Well, Romell. Far be it from me to stand in the way of your progress. If you've received a competitive offer, it would be in your best interest to take it."

"I agree."

Stevenson now pressed the intercom. "Bonnie, Mr. Goodwin will be leaving us. Drop everything and draft his letter of resignation. Then, bring it to his desk for signature."

Bonnie's voice buzzed through the static. "I don't believe I heard you correctly, sir."

"Type up a letter of resignation for Romell and bring it to him to sign. That'll be all, Bonnie." Stevenson motioned toward the empty leather chair across from the massive desk that held leather accessories, framed photos of his smiling wife and kid, a pencil and pen set, a clock, business card holder, books and bookends, and paper weights but no papers. All that time I had been in his office, I didn't even realize I remained standing. "Have a seat,

Romell, so that we can discuss your severance package. I'm sure we can come up with a practical solution," he said.

And after I sat, he got to the point immediately, "Now, since you are leaving us, what I propose is this...."

That was when I saw who he really was. The funny thing was I thought I had Stevenson's support. I was only patient for so long because he kept reassuring me that if I waited a little while longer, he would make things happen for me. After-the-next-quarter turned into after-the-New-Year and then, after-the-reorganization. Stevenson didn't seem cutthroat like the other partners. He seemed timid, without backbone. Whenever I'd pull his coattail to question him about my promotion, he'd smile and nervously make me another promise. "Just hang in there, and I'll see what I can do for you." I trusted that. But, I now realize there are no allies in this business. I got a better severance package for transitioning "all my clients" to Ian's team. Maybe the plan all along was for them to jack me for my contacts.

I was slumped at my desk, when I felt a rub on my back. I lifted my head. Bonnie had made it over with the letter. She was a middle-aged blond who still had a decent figure. She had been the secretary for over twenty years even though she was probably sharper than half the guys on the floor. She was like a second mother. She placed the letter in front of me. I looked at the fancy linen paper. Bonnie removed her cat-eye bifocals and rested them on her blouse. Her voice was soft but stern. "You don't have to do this. Don't let him force your hand."

"Why waste more time?"

Now she leaned down and whispered. "A friend of mine is an employee rights attorney. You'd have a pretty strong discrimination case. Fight this."

I knew I could fight it, but if I called myself trying to battle it out with Livings & Moore in court, my name wouldn't mean shit on Wall Street. Where else would I go? I shook my head and said, "Thanks, but no thanks. Can I borrow that pen?"

She sighed, pulled the felt-tipped pen from behind her ear, and as I signed the letter, she said, "I don't understand you."

"I know, but I'm gonna miss you, Mrs. Sutton." I handed her the letter and gave her a kiss on the cheek. Her blue eyes were glossy.

Stevenson's door was only a few feet away from my desk. Right before she entered his office with that letter, I overheard Bonnie say, "This breaks my heart."

Of course, my security escort came, a big, burly brother, looking like he was prepared to do someone some physical harm. By then, I had already ejected my computer's hard drive and swapped it for the blank one. I grabbed my stuff and headed to the door. As I passed Ian's desk, he was singing, "Another One Bites the Dust." I didn't lose my cool. Instead of continuing right on out though, I stopped, parked my box, and stepped to him. I then smiled and said, "Ian, this firm is full of sneaky, no talent, little dick mutherfuckers. You'll definitely fit in." After grabbing my nuts, I said, "Obviously, I don't." I then picked up my box and proceeded to the Exit. The security guard was no real threat. He looked at me, but didn't say a word. As he walked behind me, I heard him laughing to himself. And even though Ian's response to what I had said was to yell out, "Good riddance!" That didn't bother me. I had already said my piece.

LOVE CHANGES

Love Changes by Eartha Watts-Hicks was published in May of 2013. In June of 2013, the debut novel was honored with the Just R.E.A.D. Literary "Game Changers" Award in the fiction category from the NYCHA branch of the NAACP. The following piece was selected from over 1,500 as finalist for the National Sexy Story Contest. This is an excerpt from chapter 41.

POOKIE'S JUKEBOX CARRIED EVERYTHING FROM eight-track tapes to CDs. The store was so narrow, customers had to squeeze past each other to get by, but it seemed much larger because the entire back wall that traveled the length of the store was mirrored. So, there we were in the R&B/Hip-Hop section of this record store where there seemed to be two of everything. Two long tables full of inventory. Two smock-wearing cashiers chewing gum and blowing bubbles. Two Romells dropping old jams into his basket. And two of me.

I plucked out shrink-wrapped jewel cases and tucked them back in place. None of which were alphabetized by title or artist, so this process was taking longer than I expected. As soon as I heard speakers thumping with the bass of Soul

II Soul's "Back to Life," I was infected. My head was bobbing, and I sang along but mainly ad-libbed.

Romell interrupted me at the best part. "Why are you making up your own words?"

I stopped flipping through the CDs for a moment and turned to him. "I love this song. This one and 'Keep it Moving,' so I don't wanna hear it because I didn't say a word when you were jumping up and down to Kris Kross." I turned and went back to searching.

"You should learn the lyrics to this song that's playing."

"What for? It is not that serious. Now, let me know when you find anything by Mary J."

"Weren't you the one who told me to pay attention to the songs a person sings if I wanna know what's on their mind?"

"That was Spider's theory. What does that have to do with anything, now?" I shook my head, humming.

Romell chuckled. "I pay attention to the songs you sing, Chocolate. Now, I'm gonna hand you a few CDs. Let's see if you can figure out what's on *my* mind." He held out two CDs. On top was the R&B group, Xscape, the first release with all its cuts. The other was an old single by SWV. I looked at Romell and shrugged. He laughed and let me in on the joke. "Chocolate, if you're tired of Spider Snyder, I've got an *Xscape* for you, and you can have this 'Right Here' if you want."

"*Xscape?*" I said. I turned to the back of the CD read down the list of titles. One of them caught my attention right away. I didn't know if

Romell was serious or where he was going with this, but if he could play this game, I could play it better. I decided to throw that title out there. "Xscape. 'With You?' I never heard that before."

He reached into the basket and handed me the other CD, pointed to a song title on the back, and said, "'Do You Want To?'"

I snatched it and flipped it over to check out the front. "Xscape? That's Off the Hook." After a quick glance at the titles I added, "'Who Can I Run To?' and 'What Can I Do?'" Then, I folded my arms. I didn't think Romell had a CD in his basket that could answer that, so I was eager to see what he was going to do next. He pulled out Mary J. Blige's new single, "Be Happy." I giggled and spread the CDs out on the table. He dipped his dimpled face low and looked into my eyes. His eyes were smiling. My heart felt warm. So, I asked, "Romell, you're saying I can escape right here with you and be happy?"

He answered by licking his lips and raising his eyebrows.

I looked away, thinking. *First, Jun Ko. Now, me? Did Romell lower his standards?* I shook my head. It was hard to admit, but Jun Ko morphed. She really did look good. I just so happened to look into the mirror across from us and I realized. *My cuteness factor went way up! I'm curvy, styling. I'm...a dime. Damn, I am a dime.* I grunted as I thought about that. Then I mumbled, "He never settles for less." I looked back at Romell. His eyes were searching. I rolled mine away, mumbling under my breath, "This dirty dog."

"What did you say?"

22

I picked up two of the CDs and handed them back to him. In a cool shot, I said, "I'm not looking for any *Xscape*."

"Well, what do you want?"

"<u>My Life</u> and TLC."

He licked his lips, moaning, "Oh, I'll give you some TLC."

That sent a chill through me but I didn't let on. I folded my arms across my chest, turned, and cut my eye at him. "'Ain't Too Proud to Beg?'" I said.

"If that's what you want." He leaned over and his breath tickled my ear as he whispered, "Pal-eese, Chocolate. Please." I shivered and giggled. And while I was taking slower breaths to try to relax myself, he put the Heavy D & The Boyz CD in my hand. "This is *Heavy*. I got <u>Nuttin' But Love</u>."

I read the song titles and narrowed my eyes, "I guess you want me to have 'Sex Wit You' and 'Spend a Little Time on Top.'" My tone was filled with attitude, but he didn't seem to notice.

He held up a Tony, Toni, Toné, and said, "Whatever You Want."

I looked at it. I couldn't believe this was happening, and I couldn't even entertain the thought of any of this because my fears were louder than his sweet-talk. I sucked my teeth and handed them all back. "I don't care if this is *Heavy*! I don't wanna have "Sex Wit You," and like I said before, I'm not looking for an Xscape," I snapped.

He slammed Tony, Toni, Toné back into the basket and pulled out the Notorious BIG's album. Now, his face was tight. He smacked the

CD down on the table in front of me. "Mia, I'm giving you 'One More Chance,' and that's a Biggie!"

"I know that's a *Biggie,* but I don't need it!" I looked around, until I saw Monica. I shoved "Don't Take it Personal" into Romell's chest and squeezed past him, storming out of the record store. At the curb, I threw my arm up to hail a taxi, wondering if I had enough for the fare. Reaching into my purse for my wallet, I noticed I didn't feel my keys. I ran my hand across the bottom. Nothing. I realized where they were. Taking a deep breath, I looked to my left. Less than half a block away a peanut vendor was roasting nuts from the cart, releasing a honey-sweet aroma, but the thought of eating the peanuts was not as appealing as the thought of hurling them at Romell and sending his ass into anaphylactic shock.

I looked back at the doorway of Pookie's just as Romell came stepping out, hands in the pockets of his black slacks, two plastic bags hanging at his left. Because he works out a lot, his posture's erect but his swagger seemed looser than ever. Still, I saw tension in his face. No dimples now, he had lockjaw. He looked at me, cockeyed. "No cab? Or did you just realize you left your keys?"

I didn't answer that, and I didn't say a word to him in the cab; I tossed my head, flinging my hair back over my shoulder, twisted my body away from him, and crossed my legs. Romell tried to get my attention by whistling Marvin Gaye's "I Want You." When that didn't work, he started pelting my feet with pellets of used chewing gum wrapped in foil, seven pieces in about ten minutes. I figured he was chewing all that gum and spitting it out just to annoy me, but I kept my back to him the entire ride and walked ahead of him into the building. We rode up to the thirty-seventh floor in separate elevators. As soon as he unlocked his door, I bolted into the living room. Even in my slim skirt and croc pumps, I was Flo Jo. My leg banged into his marble cocktail table, sending it spinning around on its axis until the halves formed a circle. I dented my shin, but I wasn't rubbing my boo-boo. I jumped right on his Slinky sofa, leaned over it, reaching until I snatched my keys up off the rug. Then I made a beeline for the door, hoping I could run right out, but he blocked my exit. When I stepped to the left, he stepped to that side. When I tried to veer to the right, he kept right in front of me. I knew then he would not let me past; I had no choice but to get in his face, "What?"

"You don't wanna be with *me*?"

I shook my head.

"You *don't* wanna be with me?"

"No, I do not!"

"You show up in stilettos and a little skirt, and you expect me to believe you don't want me?"

"I did this for Spider."

"Well, Spider isn't here now. Is he? And, what about your poem?"

"What about it? I wanted you to know how I feel."

"Oh, so you admit you have feelings for me?"

25

"Pah–leese, Romell! That poem is about your situation."

"My situation, huh?"

"Yeah, that's the perfect solution."

"If you think you and I hookin' up would be the perfect solution, why don't you just say you want me?"

"Are you mental?"

"How long have you wanted me, Mia? How long?"

"Now, I *know* you've lost it. What makes you think I want *you?*"

"Your poem! I've got it right here." He patted himself down, pulled a page out of his back pocket and unfolded it in front of me. "There! You say all through this how you're gonna melt my fears away and how you're gonna make me feel."

I looked, reading aloud halfheartedly, "Chocolate Love every day can melt your fears away and have you feeling new. That's what Chocolate can do." Then, I shook my head. "And?"

He smacked his baldhead, paced and then, banged the back of it into the wall. "Chocolate, your last name is Love!"

"So? I wrote this to motivate you to embrace black love."

"Stop it. The only black Love you want me to embrace is you."

Now, I read the whole thing through. I could see how he could make that assumption. The words "Chocolate" and "Love" were both capitalized all the way through the poem, but I didn't do that intentionally. That connection didn't even occur to me when I jotted the lines down; my mind was in a totally different place. I laughed, but he didn't see humor in this, at all. His face was as stiff as steel.

I tried to explain. "I know how this looks, Romell, but that wasn't the meaning behind this. I meant chocolate as opposed to vanilla or any other flavor. Chocolate is a metaphor for black, and Love is just love, the emotion. Not my last name. That's just a coincidence."

"This ain't no coinki-dink! I told you once before. You won't be happy until I'm with a woman who's your height, your weight, and your complexion. What I should have said is you won't be happy, until I'm with *you*. Why won't you just admit it?"

"Hello! I am in a relationship with Spider. Remember him? Real tall, kinda goofy, I *love* him. Seriously, I was not coming on to you."
He stood, huffing and puffing for a moment, then looked at me hard. "Did you eat any peanuts?"

"No! What the hell kind of question is—"

I didn't finish my sentence. The next thing I knew, I felt his warm tongue, stroking mine and tickling the roof of my mouth. I heard the crackling of plastic when Romell's CD bags hit the carpet. Then, my bag dropped to the carpet, and I backed all the way to the wall, but the lower half of me began to wind as if it had a mind of its own. He grabbed my behind, pulled me into him, and boy oh boy. Now, when I walked in on Romell and Jun Ko, and saw him in those see-through drawers, I knew then: he wasn't packing peanuts there, either. Now that he was fully hard, I knew he could poke a hole in me if I let him, but still something inside me was aching for it.

I was so aroused, but it was as if the backs of my hands were glued to the wall. I couldn't bring myself to wrap my arms around him. To do so would've meant I was causing this to happen. As it stood, Romell initiated this. *He* was kissing *me*. Everything I was doing was involuntary. I wasn't stopping this, but I wasn't causing this, either. Technically, I wasn't responding. Kissing him back was only a reflex, a natural reaction to the stroke of his tongue, and the taste of spearmint, so *he* was kissing *me*. What I was feeling in my stomach I had no control over. This was my logic, and so by virtue of me keeping my hands to that wall and not "touching" him under any circumstances, I was *not guilty*.

Then, his hands started creeping their way up under my skirt. His lips left mine, traveled down my neck, and back up to my ear. "Chocolate, I need you," he whispered. I felt a jolt in my stomach—fear—next, my panties slipping off my behind. I opened one eye and saw Spider's face for a split second. That sent a chill through me, because in that instant, just like in our earlier staring match, Spider's hazel eyes bore into me. I shut mine tight now, but in my head, I could still hear his voice accusing, "If Romell is not in your bed, he's definitely on your mind."

Romell's face returned to mine. I felt his warm breath on my lips. He was panting, so was I. There was something in his eyes I'd never seen before. It scared me, because this part of me was supposed to belong to Spider. At Pookie's

Jukebox, between those mirrors, it looked like there was two of me. Now, staring into Romell's eyes, I wished there were. He closed them and then moved in to kiss again, but I sealed my lips. Still he licked, enticing me to open. He felt so good and smelled so good, but I pressed my lips tighter. I had to. My conscience was taunting me.

Romell backed up. It looked as if his eyes were reading mine. He smirked. I watched his eyes grow wide, him moisten his lips and then, wink. Now, I was totally confused. I had no clue what to expect until I watched his head take a slow descent. I lost my breath and almost suffocated as Romell gave me a gentle nibble where Spider's mouth had never been. But, if this were to happen, there would be no way I could claim *this* was involuntary. No, if Romell went down on me, I had to be a willing participant; there was no disputing that. And quite honestly, I was more curious than anything else, especially since I always had this inkling that sexually, Romell would just blow me away. So, deep down inside, there was this secret place in me that always longed for this, even if it were only just once. This was not Spider, but I always wanted to experience a man's tongue *there*. But then again, this wasn't just any man. This was Romell. He was the one collecting my panties in his teeth. This was Romell dragging them down my thigh. I was already tingling. This was Romell, not Spider. My panties were now at my ankles, and I didn't know what to do.

CONVERSE

Utter89 [5:52 AM]: Hi there.

TiffanyDiamond [5:52 AM]: Hey Mike!

Utter89 [5:54 AM]: Diamond, are you free this Sunday?

TiffanyDiamond [5:55 AM]: Yeah, why?

Utter89 [5:56 AM]: I have a function to go to. Now you have another excuse to wear the sexy bridesmaid dress you were telling me about.

TiffanyDiamond [5:57 AM]: You want me to go with you?

Utter89 [5:57 AM]: That's the plan.

TiffanyDiamond [5:57 AM]: Like meet in person???

Utter89 [5:57 AM]: Problem?

TiffanyDiamond [5:59 AM]: Not really. Just awkward. I get friended by guys on FB all the time.

Utter89 [6:00 AM]: I'm sure.

TiffanyDiamond [6:01 AM]: Not for nothing, but I see your pix. You're not bad looking. What made you decide to chat me up?

Utter89 [6:02 AM]: You shine, Diamond.

TiffanyDiamond [6:02 AM]: Diamonds sparkle.

Utter89 [6:03 AM]: Lol. No seriously, I just wanted to get to know you better and see that pretty smile for myself.

TiffanyDiamond [6:03 AM]: Don't you have like 2000 FB friends? And most of your friends are female. Couldn't you ask some other smiling face with a disposable dress to go to this thing?

Utter89 [6:04 AM]: I tried but Halle Berry is busy.

TiffanyDiamond [6:04 AM]: LMBAO

Utter89 [6:05 AM]: So you meet guys on FB all the time?

TiffanyDiamond [6:06 AM]: Yeah stalkers, spammers, and identity thieves.

Utter89 [6:06 AM]: ROTFLMBAO

Utter89 [6:08 AM]: For real?

TiffanyDiamond [6:08 AM]: Yup. Friend requests. DMs. Nobody calls me offline, tho.

TiffanyDiamond [6:08 AM]: The last time I met a FB guy, it didn't go well.

Utter89 [6:09 AM]: Stalker type?

TiffanyDiamond [6:09 AM]: Not at all. We were supposed to meet at Starbucks in Times Square. He showed up but pretended he didn't see me.

Utter89 [6:10 AM]: How do you know he was pretending? He probably didn't recognize you.

TiffanyDiamond [6:13 AM]: I was the only black girl in the place! I called his name twice but he walked out.

TiffanyDiamond [6:14 AM]: I drank 3 cappuccinos waiting for him. You know how much those things cost!!!

TiffanyDiamond [6:14 AM]: I tried to send him a message when I got home but he blocked me. :o(

Utter89 [6:14 AM]: That must suck.

TiffanyDiamond [6:16 AM]: Like a vacuum cleaner!

Utter89 [6:18 AM]: I don't understand why some dudes do that?

TiffanyDiamond [6:20 AM]: I do. My hair is not long anymore. I tried to save money by getting a perm at a beauty school. I walked out with my hair in a bag. Either he had a problem with my profile picture or he didn't like what he saw in person. But that's ok. Experiences like that are humbly.

Utter89 [6:21 AM]: Maybe, but I don't think you need to be humbled. I love your energy.
TiffanyDiamond [6:22 AM]: :-D
TiffanyDiamond [6:22 AM]: okay
TiffanyDiamond [6:22 AM]: I'm taking the disposable dress
TiffanyDiamond [6:22 AM]: to the cleaners
TiffanyDiamond [6:22 AM]: on my way to work!!!
TiffanyDiamond [6:22 AM]: Let's meet somewhere public.
TiffanyDiamond [6:23 AM]: Details please! 917-555-7223.
Utter89 [6:27 AM]: My battery is charging.
Utter89 [6:27 AM]: Check email. ttl

Mike and Diamond first connected in the *I Still Love Neo Soul Facebook* group. Mike quoted Revelations 3:17; Diamond a true blue Jill Scott fan was the only one that "liked" it. He sent her a friend request. Diamond accepted and messaged him a smiley face. The very next morning, seeing she was online, he sent her this Facebook chat message:

:o)

Hi there! Thanks for the add!

Their conversations began and had, thus far, been instant messages either through Facebook and AIM or text messages occasionally on just about every topic. Diamond knew of the Wacky Pack trading cards Mike began collecting. He knew her favorite colors were pumpkin and teal, and that she secretly dreamed of being an interior decorator.

Diamond was enrolled in nursing school. Her grandmother and two of her aunts were retired nurses, and often bragged of the who's who of patients they'd had under their care. Diamond reluctantly chose the field only after her high school guidance counselor discouraged her ambitions by saying, "A straight black woman could never earn a living as a decorator." When Diamond asked why not, the white woman told her, "Wealthy people don't hire black decorators. And black people don't hire decorators, at all." Diamond shared this with Mike.

Just 22 years old, Mike had lived long enough to understand and accept his own shortcomings, but at the same time he refused to be limited by them or anyone else's expectations. His challenges were his to face and his alone. He would never make the mistake of allowing someone else to define him or put him in a box. His response:

> **Utter89 [11:53 PM]:** Don't believe that.
> **Utter89 [11:54 PM]:** Take a class somewhere. Somebody said something similar to
> **Utter89 [11:54 PM]:** Obama.
> **Utter89 [11:54 PM]:** There will always be haters!
> **Utter89 [11:55 PM]:** Don't give them a headstart.

Diamond changed the subject. But after that exchange, Mike tried to encourage her however he could. He would periodically email her links to BHG's and HGTV's decorating sites, information on workshops, color wheels, Small Space Storage articles, ethnic design books on Amazon.com, and finally Cecil Hayes's web page.

He thought they had gotten to know each other well over the course of three months, but in all actuality, some things never came up in conversation. Each disclosed what little they felt comfortable sharing about themselves, just enough to keep the other interested. And after only viewing profile pictures, strategically chosen to capture them at their best, grinning and posed, Mike would finally meet Diamond face to face. Not once did she ask why he never called.

On a rainy Sunday afternoon in June, Diamond insisted on meeting outdoors. Mike sent her a text, suggesting she meet him in the Three Bears Playground on the south side of the Metropolitan Museum. He arrived half an hour ahead of time. The playground clearing was as fragrant as if he were standing in the thick labyrinth of grass, trees, and bushes. The last time he had been here was for a photo shoot. The designer had him wearing shorts in the middle of January, and as the crowd swelled with giggling children, he felt more and more like a spectacle. In this downpour at present, there wasn't a single child in sight and the few passersby proceeded hurriedly past, faces masked with the same expression, Manhattan apathy. Surrounded by benches, but without a dry place to sit, Mike stood beneath his umbrella, braving the elements. Despite the heat, wind, and rainfall, he waited patiently by the bronze statue.

For lunch earlier he had driven to a well-known Cantonese restaurant on Broadway. The waiter served his meal with a fortune cookie. After reading this fortune, "A romantic evening awaits you tonight," Mike ate his Teriyaki Chicken and mixed vegetables, discarding the onions. Now holding a mixed bouquet of dry Eucalyptus tinted pumpkin and teal, he hoped the dye wouldn't bleed on his shirt or his rented tux. And as Central Park's foliage released a sweet, somewhat pungent fragrance into the haze, Mike also hoped the scent he smelled was not pollen.

Before long, a large blue and white umbrella with printed lettering turned the corner onto the approaching path. The busty, short waisted girl was no Halle Berry, but she was uniquely pretty. Mike watched her steps splash through puddles. Stiletto heels on her sandals seemed to make her strut like Beyoncé. The damp teal gown clung to her legs and told him exactly who she was. He could also tell she was embracing her inner artist, at least on some level. This Diamond was decorated with a lot of costume jewelry: large jewel earrings, a necklace, and bracelets on both wrists like a goddess. She reached Mike, smiling when their eyes met. He smiled back. Her haircut was chic enough; the long bang, unnecessary and obviously a wig of some sort. It cascaded into her eyes. After running her fingers through and tucking the piece behind her ear, Diamond said, "You're early."

Mike responded, "And you're even p-p-prettier in p-p-person."

"What was that?"

Mike felt his eye jumping. He cleared his throat, closed his eyes, and took a deep breath but now felt spasms take over the whole right side of his face. He tried again. "You're p-p-prettier in p-p-person." This time a dragging noise followed his words.

Mike kept his eyes shut for a moment, hoping this would pass, but felt his face and even his neck twitching. When Mike opened his eyes, he saw that Diamond was some distance away. She had bolted. He caught up to her just as she reached Fifth Avenue, where she hesitated, as if deciding between directions. He touched her shoulder, asking, "W-w-where are you going? What's wrong?"

"Stay away from me! Who are you?"

"It's me! M-m-mike!"

"What scam are you trying to pull? Who put you up to this? You are not the guy I've been talking to on Facebook!"

"Yes, I am!" Mike was emphatic, but he could tell Diamond did recognize him from his Facebook photos by the expression on her face; she looked perplexed.

She studied him for a moment but then, without warning, took off heading uptown in the direction of the Subway station. Again, he went after her. Earlier, when she first laid eyes on Mike standing by the statue, she liked what she saw. He knew that because she smiled instantly. His stature and strong, lean physique helped pay his way through college. Once sought after by skate/surf advertisers for his body type and length of woolly hair, Mike's best feature was his smile. His work ethic was such that Tourette's Syndrome had never hindered him from landing assignments, nor did his stuttering. His agency would cast him in commercials, including principal roles with lines, still spawning residual checks two years later. That career, though brief, was good while it lasted.

Mike was now focusing on his own endeavors. Digitally manipulating his sketches and then integrating the designs with text was something he was very passionate about. Everything bound inside of him because of his communication challenge—all those ideas— would burst forth onto any blank canvas. And critics raved because such imagination was not expected of someone like him, someone with...afflictions. He became a spokesperson but not by choice. Mike wanted recognition, but what he wanted more than anything was genuine acceptance. He didn't need anyone's pity. To indulge was to stunt growth of any kind. So much of his childhood was spent wishing his conditions away. Now, thanks to the veil of technology, Mike not only had a blank canvas, but a way to ward off prejudices, a chance for others to get to know him. Texting, instant messaging, and emails allowed Mike to be what he always longed to be, just another person. He could interact as his true clever and charismatic self, without the need to explain or apologize. In a sense, this was his freedom.

His tics were sporadic and totally unpredictable. His tics were something he tried to regulate through diet and exercise. Most likely triggered now by something in the environment, probably pollen, his tics were usually not severe. Mike knew this. Plus Mike knew, at least in theory, how to control his stuttering: through breathing exercises; thinking about what he intended to say; concentrating on where his tongue should be placed for hard consonants;

and minding his p's, b's, d's, m's, t's, and w's. *Relax, breathe easy, speak slowly. Relax, breathe easy, speak slowly. Simple. So simple.* These steps played out well when Mike read lines from scripts, preview copies he'd mark up for pauses and breaths. But who could remember all that in a situation like this?

"I *am* Mike. B-b-but if you want, I'll take you home," he said.

Diamond stopped and turned around. "In your Porsche?"

Mike nodded. Afterward, he couldn't stop his head from shaking. This too was involuntary. To disguise it, he turned his collar up. Then, he reached into his jacket pocket, pulled out his iPhone, and plugged his earphones into his ears. His songs were on shuffle. Jay Z was playing. Mike, annoyed by such eloquence, turned the volume down.

"You ain't driving no Porsche! I must look like a fool! I don't believe this! Everybody on Facebook is bogus! Everyone pretends to be someone else! Why do I get all the goons? All the gargoyles. All the frogs, trolls...and retards."

Her last comment struck a nerve. Mike was so appalled; his iPhone slipped out of his hand and hit the ground. He quickly picked it up, dried it off, and examined it. Seeing the spider web that had spread across the glass screen, he screamed and then yelled at her, "I said I'll take you home! Didn't I?"

"Show me your keys. You drive a Porsche? Show me your car keys!"

Mike knew why she demanded to see his key. He reached into his pocket but pulled his hand out empty. "No, I'm not doing that," he said.

"Oh, so I'm just supposed to believe you? Right?" Diamond threw her arms up in disgust. "This is somethin' else," she said. "I kept giving you my cell phone number, but you would never call. A damn shame, because I really did kind of like you. You or whoever that was."

Mike threw the flowers down and stepped over them on his way to the curb. Squeezing between two parked cars, he blew a loud, shrill whistle. A yellow taxi swerved to him. Mike opened the door for Diamond and said, "Get in."

She shook her head. "I don't have cabfare!"

"I got it," he said.

Diamond looked at him with pursed lips, but she squeezed her way through to the taxicab, closed her umbrella, and sat. The wet umbrella had rust stains and exposed spokes. Mike recognized the logo on it. It was a promotional giveaway from a bank that went out of business years ago. The only word that had not completely peeled off the thing was the word TRUST. And as pretty as she was, when Diamond threw her arms up in the air, during that split second, he noticed that she had neglected to shave under her arms, and here she was wearing a very elegant, teal, strapless gown. Mike laughed to himself. Diamond sat with her arms crossed now and continued to brood, "No one on Facebook is ever who they say they are. Bogus," she said. "I should've known something was up with you. Not one time did you call me and try to conversate. Not one time. Now I know why."

If nothing else, Mike had the power to decide

for himself, which battles to pick and choose. He shrugged his shoulders and closed the door behind her. He rapped on the driver's window, retrieved his wallet, and reached into it for one of the larger bills. He made sure he slipped it into the taxi driver's hand and discreetly instructed him, "Take her home. Keep the rest." He then took one last look at Diamond, and without any reoccurrence of tics or twitching, he said, "The word is converse. My last name is Longmeadow. Google me."

Because Mike was so angry, he did not stutter. He simply stepped out of the way and let the taxi pull off. Mike's car was parked just a few feet away. He now fished his key from his pocket. It was the Panamera's key, a flash drive. Resembling a toy car, it was embossed with Porsche's crest.

He figured Diamond had never read graphic novels, knew nothing about his fan pages, and had never visited any of his blogs or websites. He knew that by the time Diamond Googled him and saw his Wikipedia entry or LinkedIn profile, she would have realized her mistake and would message him an apology. He also knew by then, he would already have blocked her. Diamond would definitely tell her next Facebook love interest about Mike and all about this situation, wondering why things like this keep happening to her, even commenting that experiences like these are "humbly." If she learned anything at all from this experience, next time she'd think before she reacts.

TORI

"Tori! Here comes the cutie," Linda yelled in her Dominican accent, as thick as gravy. "Ten dollars, right?"

Tori snatched open her purse for her brush and quickly fixed her bangs. "Today, I'll make it twenty."

"Bet! I could stand to get my nails did," said Dae. "Get my money ready!"

"You mean *my* money," Linda said.

At that, Tori grabbed her purse again and reached into a fat, white, bank envelope for the twenty dollar bill she sat on top of her cash register. She then wrapped the handbag back in its plastic bag and returned it to the cabinet. She was willing to cough up some of the cash she had been diligently socking away to buy her first automobile from her stingy older brother, Oscar. Oscar, whom she always called O.B., had found success working as an entertainment lawyer and would only part with his used Audi, if the price was right. This Audi was a convertible, so in lieu of her modeling dream, Tori's classes at community college and her scheduled hours at The Friendly Farmer became her life.

The Friendly Farmer was a specialty market located on the Upper West Side of Manhattan. They offered organic produce, imported wines, cold cuts, and cheeses, free range poultry, fresh wild fish, baked breads, and gourmet entrees at an open buffet style salad bar. It was one of the few markets left that not only offered a wide assortment of every fruit and vegetable imaginable, customers could choose any one of the wicker baskets hanging from the ceiling to have customized with exotic items, packaged, and shipped via FedEx to any location in the country.

Bob, the store manager, was an aging black man from Brooklyn. No store in his neighborhood even remotely resembled this. Still, he worked sixteen hours a day to ensure this place lived up to chain's reputation of *a truly pleasurable shopping experience.* This market's clientele was used to being catered to. They could order online and conveniently have their groceries delivered to them in an hour's time, if they were within a five mile radius. But most were attracted to The Friendly Farmer's splendor, which was why the items sold here were overpriced, and why Bob always paid his staff more handsomely than other local markets. And though it was the girls from the outer boroughs who lacked tact, they were always on time and their registers never came up short. Bob dabbed at his forehead with his handkerchief. He usually blamed his graying hair on the three teenaged granddaughters that he and his wife had been raising, right now he felt his granddaughters only deserved credit for half. Walking toward the deli section, Bob yelled over his shoulder to the giggling cashiers, "Girls, no flirting with the customers! I mean it!"

The cashiers would never outwardly undermine their manager's authority, but his warning fell on deaf ears. The thought ringing in their heads was unanimous. *Shut up, Bob.* This trio formed an odd clique. Linda, the eldest, was a nineteen year old, but very petite and very pretty. Her favorite color was pink and she could almost always be found wearing something floral or lace. Dae was a Brooklyn girl. Her rainbow colored eye makeup was an obvious sign that she was aspiring makeup artist. Her skirts were always too short. Her hair was always worn up to reveal the tattoo on the back of her neck in fancy letters, "Jayquan's." Dae was only eighteen, but so curvaceous most usually assumed she was in her thirties. Tori was plain and simple, the tallest and the thinnest. Underneath her smock, she was dressed in a plain white t-shirt and nondescript blue jeans. Her belt was canvas and tied in a knot. Her nickel plated earrings were in her pocket, because metal made her itch.

If ever a guy could ever be perfect, "the cutie" seemed to be the one. He had deep brown skin, bright eyes, and gorgeous features. But, at the bridge of his nose, his only noticeable flaw: the odd hump that made him resemble a snapping turtle. Still, taller than tall, he was chiseled. The girls followed him around the store with their eyes until he disappeared behind the display of French bread. As shy as Tori was, she had been panting like a puppy. As was always the case, it wasn't until after he'd leave the supermarket that she could even start to breathe again. She was willing to cough up hard earned money, because she had never worked up the nerve to speak to this guy. Hence, the twenty dollars that was now in place atop her cash register, next to the half slice of lemon she used to create traction on her fingertips. A trick she learned to prevent miscounting new bills.

The cutie never said a word to anyone. He would literally whisk in and out, but in a matter of seconds would manage to transform Tori's somber disposition. The cutie always carried a huge duffle bag. He always wore expensive sneakers and matching athletic gear, never sweats. He always wore sports tights and shirts, always seemed to be on his way to or from the gym, and always went straight to the dairy section. Now, he reappeared, rushing to the front with muscle milk and a half dozen carton of pre-cooked hardboiled eggs.

Linda was on register one, she raised her hand and motioned with her fingers. Dae was closest to him, on register two; she frantically waved him over. The girls looked at each other and then at the customer. At same time, both screamed, "I'm open!"

The cutie shook his head and changed direction, walking away from the overzealous cashiers straight to Tori's register, the farthest away. He laid his groceries down and pulled out his wallet.

Tori took a deep breath and said, "Credit or Debit?"

"Cash."

She sighed, "Always cash."

He looked at her and asked, "Why? Is there a problem?"

Tori shook her head, leaned in, and whispered, "Can I ask you a personal question?"

"That depends on the question," he said. He looked at her face, seeing her full lips had spread into a warm smile, he caved. "Okay, what's your question?"

"How old are you?"

He laughed. "For real? That's what you want to ask me? That's cute. I haven't been asked that in a long time. But to answer your question, I'm twenty-eight." He looked at her face again, expecting a smile, but there was none. Her disappointment was obvious.

Tori handed him the plastic bag with his groceries and placed his change in his hand. "Here you go, sir. Twelve dollars and three cents. Thank you for shopping at The Friendly Farmer. Have a nice day."

"Did I say something wrong?"

"No. Not really. It's just that I was hoping you were a lot younger."

"Really? Well, how old are you?"

"I'm seventeen."

"Oh, I see. You're still in high school?"

"No, actually, I'm in college. My birthday is next month."

"That's not so bad. What's your name?"

"Tori."

"Well, nice to meet you, Miss Tori. Are you into sports?" He could tell from her reaction that his question had put her on the defensive.

Tori had taken a step back. Her body language had changed and so did her voice. "What kind of sports?" She asked, looking up and down at him.

"Whoa, girl! Don't get the wrong idea. That's not a loaded question." He laughed. "You have no clue who I am, do you?"

Tori looked at the twenty dollar bill atop her register. She had been hoping for six months that he'd come in and pay by credit card just once so she could find that out, but now was her chance to hear it from him. She shook her head, and said, "No, but I should. I would at least like to know your name."

"Guillermo," He said. "My name is Guillermo."

"Guillermo?"

"Yes. Guillermo."

"You don't look like a Guillermo. You don't look Spanish at all."

"But, I am. I'm Dominican. My last name is Cruz."

"You don't have no accent!"

"I was born in the Brooklyn," he said. And then he bent to whisper in her ear. "Miss Tori, would you like to go out with me? I would really like to sit and talk with you somewhere."

"Maybe. I don't know. I need some time to think about that." Tori drew a breath and said, "Yes! Definitely! I get off at five. I'll be standing outside that door at 5:02."

Guillermo laughed. "I'm heading somewhere now, and I'll be tied up for a while. I was thinking maybe we could get together tomorrow night. Are you free?"

"I will be!" Tori turned the receipt over in his hand and wrote her cell phone number on the back of it.

He smiled and said, "I'll call you." Guillermo started towards the door, but then he stopped, walk back to Tori, and whispered in her ear, "Can I ask you a personal question?"

"Sure."

"Why are you so eager to go out with me?"

"Because you're cute," she said. His question seemed to be the most ridiculous in the world. Tori had to bite her tongue to refrain from saying, "Duh!"

Guillermo smiled, nodded, and said, "Good answer. I think you're cute, too."

Tori smiled, saying, "Call me," further emphasizing by bending her fingers into the hand gesture. *Call me.* Her eyes followed Guillermo out the storefront and everyone pretending to be preoccupied stopped and craned their necks watching him leave. And as soon as he was out of sight, the girls exploded into laughter.

Tori pick up the twenty and stuff it in her bra. "I'll have you know that I'll be the future Mrs. Cruz. And that information didn't cost me a dime," she said.

"Cruz? He's Latino?"

"Yeah, Linda. He's Dominican like you. His first name is Guillermo."

Dae shook her head and said, "I would've never guessed in a million years he was Spanish."

"Gosh, Dae! The correct term is Latino. Now, does *that* cutie live in *this* neighborhood?"

"In this neighborhood? Of course not!" Tori said. "I'd bet any amount of money that he works in that gym upstairs."

"Speaking of any amount money, you see me and little Miss Latina here. We are your partners in crime. We were your accomplices. We helped orchestrate this thing here. Not only should you be thanking us, you should be hooking us up with ten dollars each."

"For what? You hookers ain't do shit."

"Gosh, that messed up!"

"That bitch know she ain't right!"

In a mock gesture, Tori took the twenty out of her bra. She grabbed her purse, unwrapped it, and returned the twenty to fat bank envelope. She then turned around and faced her girls. And now, quoting her older brother, she said, "Sue me."

DREAMING OF FOREVER

HE ASKED, "WHAT DO YOU WANT?"

I'd already crawled out from under the comforter and was trying to creep away, but he had long arms. This man reached out, hooked his palm around my hip, pulled me back into bed, and squeezed me. He squeezed, like I was the softest thing he'd ever held onto. As for what I thought he'd just asked, I had to think it out. "For breakfast? I'm in the mood for a nine grain bagel, an apple, and a cup of green tea with honey."

"I'm not talking food. You got me. Period. Now, tell me what you want. And tell me the truth."

If this was a test, I didn't know the answer. Truth was, I had only known what I didn't want and anything else besides food was even harder to fathom. "You can...rub my shoulders. You can keep grilling me steaks, tender and marinated in the Mesquite rub like you always do. And, when you get a chance, help me clear all that junk out the basement. You can fix my dishwasher and find the right sized washing machine hose to fit that faucet. Just little things. You can drive me around. And stay around. And don't change. Don't switch up on me. Don't introduce me to something beautiful, just to have me killing myself, dying to get it back."

He'd be warm, but he'd have me trembling. He was new. He'd feel strong and gorgeous, even more beautiful with the lights out, and he'd hold me close enough for me to feel as if I were basking in bathwater, his warm skin and heartbeat through the charmeuse. And I could swear I feel fear seeping out of me. His lips, at some point, would press against my hand, and he wouldn't need to say another word. He'd rocked me. In a dark bedroom, without whimpers or sniffles, I'd ease my head to the side, so tears could drain into the pillow without him noticing. I knew he'd treat my heart like it was a robin's egg. He was my man. All mine. The last and final Mayor of Willacoochee because somehow, I already knew he would always be enough.

Sometimes we face tough choices. Sometimes we have no choice but to exercise damage control and fix a problem we did not cause, because unbeknownst to us, we are thrown into confusion. This was obvious, because it felt right.

His voice would be clear, always warm and sweet. It would feel like caramel syrup. The face, a bit fuzzy. I could tell he has a large form. The face was always fuzzy, every single time, whether I slept for hours or drifted catching glimpses of him in a catnap. Maybe that is why I was so eager to find him, or rather so eager to rush to hope and assume that every man in the meantime was this man, my man, "the one" I was meant to be with. *Well, maybe he's fuzzy because he has a beard.* That was my best guess. I would never fully "see" him but could always sense this incredible energy. Being with him in those moments, I'd float like I was lighter on the inside. This would be the man I'd spend forever with, not just some phantom, and I could never figure out why I instinctively knew every, single morning after. But I always felt the fact that I only knew him from a dream, pathetic.

The worst part about single life is the loneliness: the dread and fear that there will never be "someone," and that sad sullen feeling that comes along with having to lick my own wounds. I'd break with Exes, pray for them and their happiness, and prosperity, and pray for my enlightenment. But then, seeing them smitten with someone else, would do nothing but make me ache inside, wondering. *Why not me? What's wrong with me?*

Why couldn't I be the happy one, with the over attentive lover, doting on me, and fawning over everything I do? Where were my walks, hand in hand into the sunset? Why did everyone I see "in love" have that "glow," but whenever I was in love I had the mean-mug, under-eye circles, bags and baggage? Looking miserable and half-dead, because I'd wind up loving that person who would rather use me like toilet tissue. And leave me with nothing left to show for our time but the wrinkles aggravation presses into a face and raggedy lingerie.

Did I have to tolerate everything to prove that I could and would love unconditionally, just so I could receive unconditional love? Was it that I needed to push past that barrier to get to the good stuff? And if so, would his commitment to me, ever mirror mine? Or did I need to approach relationships with caution and bylaws? *If you want me to do such and such, you must abide by the following terms, and conditions....*

Was it a possibility that love was just meant to be heartache, imbalanced and unfair: only those lovers who first chase and make promises, next torture me with the most delicious sex, then lie and neglect, before antagonizing me and belittling me, as if I had never been worthy? And then soon enough, someone new would pursue and make promises. *Why try?* Even thinking about the cycle was sickening. What's the point when ALL men only seem to want what's next, fresh, and new? Forget suitable! Is there, was there, or will there ever be one who's even satiable?

These were the things that kept me up into the wee hours until worries would segue, resurrecting my recurring dream. At least there, I'd sleep warm and safely, in the arms of my very own king. *Does this man exist or are they all the same? Is there any such thing as a trustworthy man? Should I continue to waste time pondering these things?*

All I knew for certain was this: I deserve someone who'd treat me right...

ESSAYS (Creative Non-fiction)

Hollywood in the Hood

I was 10 years old during the summer of 1981, when I flew to Chicago on a vacation with my Nana. We stayed with her sister, Eunora, who lived on the South side. That's where, I'd met my cousin Mashaun "the movie star" who was two years older than me. She had a minor role in The Marva Collin's Story, portraying Cecily Tyson's daughter, but she was the BIGGEST star in the world to me, because she was my cousin. That summer my cousin gave me the gift of rhythm. My two left feet learned how to do "The Gigolo" to Earth Wind and Fire's "Let's Groove." I learned how to do The Pop, the precursor to The Electric Boogie to the song "Numbers" by Kraftwerk. And I was never a wallflower again. After that....

In 1983 though, I remember staring out my window to watch the neighborhood boys dance. I lived in Mitchell Houses, in the very same building (and on the very same floor), where the DJ/producer for the Force MCs/MDs resided, the 10th floor. The loud music I most often overheard, though, was almost always from outside. My building was also the same building, where the Beat Street Breakers perfected their routines, every chance they could get. They were always spinning around on the ground floor, right outside my window and they all knew my name, because I went to the corner store often. And every time I did, I'd first stand in the doorway of the building, and say, "Excuse me. Can you please move your mat?" I was referring to a huge slab of cardboard they had pieced together to fit perfectly into the landing in front of our doorway. They would pause their boombox, which would more than likely be blaring "Beat Box" by The Art of Noise. Then, one of them would grab their mat, pick it up, and step aside, as the rest of them would watch me walk down the ramp. They were respectful.

Hood boys enjoy sister-girl sass when the weather's warm and shorts are short. I happened to have cute girlfriends, who happened to wear short shorts. Me and my sister-girlfriends had a ball watching Harry Belafante Presents: Beat Street. Harry Belafonte did what the producers of The Marva Collins Story did, he recruited neighborhood kids for the film. I loved being able to point out the dancers in the crew and name them one by one. From watching them just outside my 10th floor window, I knew which ones, just popped; which ones were only Breakers; which did both; who did the best Up-rock, and who did the best Windmill. Rule of thumb, if they were Puerto Rican, they were usually better at Breaking and the UpRock. If they were black, they were usually better at the Electric Boogie, Back Slide, Poppin' and Pop-Lockin'. The "star" from our neighborhood, was a talented brown-skinned Breaker and he, too, was Puerto Rican.

The truth is, I only went to see that movie, so that I could go see all of them on the giant screen. Knowing them and what they were doing in its own little way, made me feel important. I, myself, was later cast in a Break Dance movie. It was supposed to be called Wild Style '85. The film project was cancelled before a scene was ever filmed.

The Bestest Model in the Whole Wide World

I'm a mother, a doting parent. Please allow me a moment to brag about my baby....

My daughter was a beautiful baby. Not only was she beautiful, she was a spirited, precocious, and boldly outspoken child before she was even 2 years old. She was wonderful! So unlike myself that I celebrated every deviation from my own personality.

I remember visiting a friend of mine who, at the time, managed a modeling agency. My daughter had just turned 4. One of the ladies on the agency's staff was previously in charge of development and recruitment at thc Ophelia deVore Charm School, the same charm school that churned out the likes of Diahann Carroll, newswoman Sue Simmons, and hip-hop/R&B artist Faith Evans. Now, as part of Silk Model Management, Shandy was responsible for the image enhancement, training, and development of fashion models. She herself, though, having the background as part of the integral leadership of the most prestigious charm school to ever service minorities in this country (and probably the world), Shandy had ambitions of starting her own beauty pageant for little black girls. This was a beautiful idea. Shandy had the support of the agency and was going to enlist the help of their top models to train these children, ages 5 to 9, to walk with poise, grace the stage and the runway.

My daughter, at the time, did not meet their age requirement. She was 4. I approached Shandy, requesting that my daughter join and explained that although she was only a 4 year-old, she was unusually advanced. And, Shandy, that wonderful woman that she was, said, "If she can learn the walk, she can do the show."

From then on, every Saturday, my daughter learned how to walk The Catwalk; how to engage the audience; all the pivots and turns—full, three-quarter, half, quarter. She soon knew stage presence and how to bring attention to the clothing.

My daughter did three fashion shows with Silk Model Management, one being at the newly constructed State Office Building on 125th Street in Harlem. By that point, Shandy had only been able to enlist two other children, a 6 year-old, and soon added, was a 12 year old. And seeing how she was always the youngest amongst the three children, showcasing with adult professional models and was absolutely adorable, my baby girl was always the show stopper. Oddly enough, once she hit the stage, she would turn on like a light bulb, place hands on her hips and sashay as well as any of the adult professionals, but in a 4 year-old package.

My baby was in and around the fashion world and amongst fashion icons. I made sure she dressed the part, by any off-priced means necessary, Daffy's, TJ Maxx, Century 21, wherever. I even was able to find a pair of patent leather Moschino ankle boots, embellished with the name in silver charm letters. Though they were two sizes too large (and stuffed with cotton), my daughter wore those little boots like she was tipping through Saks Fifth Avenue. And her fashion cohorts were stunned to see my little one wearing this tiny replica of these two thousand dollar boots. And at just $59.99 plus tax, thanks to Daffy's! I probably paid for them over time, knowing me. But I had them purchased just in time for her stage performance and to coordinate with her black velvet jumper dress and matching red wool blazer with black velvet collar. And in a fashion show down in the East Village, it was when my preschooler was wearing that outfit, that she surprised me the most. While walking across the stage, she unbuttoned her blazer, and in one fluid motion, let it drop, flung it over her shoulder on one finger and proceeded with a full spin...while smiling. I was so amazed that I was completely pulled out of the moment. I jumped up, pointed to the stage, and said, "Who taught her that?" That was a mystery I never solved.

Now, these shows were causing quite the stir after a year and a half, but Shandy was beginning to realize that she was not getting parents eager enough to enroll their children. She had so passionately been trying to put together a beauty pageant, but decided to table the idea. Meanwhile my daughter was left in limbo with this Supermodel catwalk skill.

Around this time, I was reading a magazine

for black entrepreneurs. They had done a full article on a modeling agency that specialized in children of color, and the agency was not Silk Model Management, but was located just a few buildings over. After seeing that article, I was inspired. I grab my baby stroller, strapped in my infant son, grabbed my camera, and went throughout the neighborhood, taking candid photos of my daughter: on the block, outside of a neighborhood church's outdoor garden, at the firehouse, in front of a fire truck. We snapped away as we strolled through the neighborhood with my baby boy in tow.

When I had gathered enough of these adorable photos, I dressed my daughter up, styled her hair into something very pretty, and we took a walk over to this children's modeling agency. As I push the stroller across the threshold and entered the suite, approaching the receptionist, I look, noticing the assortment of beautiful kids pictured on the walls. I also noticed that only two of those children were darker brown skinned. Of those two, one had a very dark complexion and natural hair that was completely straight, silky but without wave, and the other was about my daughter's complexion, dark brown with cobalt blue eyes. All the rest, it was difficult to determine their nationalities. But the owner (as pictured in the magazine photo) and receptionist before me were both brown, black women who looked like me.

I shook off, any second thoughts, smiled at the receptionist and said, "Hi, I'm here with my daughter and I would like to possibly schedule an interview. We have Polaroids and she has experience."

The receptionist looked up from her desk at us. With a blank face and in a nasty tone she said, "She's not what we're looking for."

I said, "My daughter has almost a year's experience doing runway. Can you please show us to someone who can watch her walk? She has an incredible walk and she's still only 5."

Again, the woman said, "She's not what we're looking for."

I now said, "Will you at least look at the pictures?"

She raised her voice, "I said she's not what we're looking for!"

Now in the stroller, my son was a beautiful infant with a soft tan complexion and chestnut eyes, not that that matters, because I really wasn't there to pitch the baby, but now I was just curious. But even when I said, "Well, what about my son?" she did not relent.

The woman rudely responded, "Him neither!"

At that point, I walked away from the receptionist, grabbed my kids and stepped out of the suite into the hall by the elevator.

My daughter now looked at me and said, "Mommy! What was wrong with that woman! She didn't look at my pictures! She didn't even let me walk! And I'm the best-est model in the whole, wide world!"

That was a defining moment. Hearing my little girl say those words, I stopped being upset. Trying not to giggle, I said to my daughter, "You're right, baby. And she's stupid! Come on! Let's go to McDonalds!"

I knew stage moms and beautiful kids had

the ability to earn an extra nickel in the 90s, picking up modeling assignments here and there. But that encounter, made me decide then and there that I was not going to sacrifice my daughter's self-esteem, not for a pretty penny or a few extra bucks.

After that, though, I did take my daughter to one model casting. Instructing her on the way, "We are only going for the free toy and to meet the Spice Girls." This was an open casting call for the Mattel Spice Girl toy commercial and they were specifically looking for girls that were Spice Girl lookalikes and guaranteeing a parting gift, a not-yet-released Spice Girl toy to each and every one of the 1500 little girls that turned out for the Manhattan open casting. My daughter was a huge fan of the Spice Girls, whether she looked like Scary Spice or not.

Now, as this collection goes to publication, my baby girl is 24 years old with all the confidence that money can't buy. She also kept that incredible runway strut. Whenever she was asked to participate in anybody's fashion show, whether in Girl Scouts, high school, college, or anywhere else, she'd turn it on. And strangely enough, she doesn't even remember where it came from.

NOTE: Today, my sister-friend Jackie Love is filling this void, training with children of all ages, hues, including those with special needs. And Jackie Love's Kids rip the runway at key fashion events here and abroad. For more information, visit her j.loveFashionschool.org. Donations can be sent via PayPal to jacquelinelv827@gmail.com.

THAT'S WHAT YOU GET FOR BEING POLITE

One late night, my cousin and I got dressed up and went to a night club that was known to be a celebrity hot spot. While we were there, all night, we were dancing and mingling with the famous and familiar. A well-known actor took a serious liking to my beautiful cousin. As a result, we were invited to the red-carpet movie premier and after party for, get this, THE BEST MAN.

We could not attend the movie premier, because she had to work, so we went straight to the after party. Very few had arrived early. So we sat on a sofa positioned behind a coffee table. On the other side of the table, was another sofa. Two young, chic, beautiful black women, much like ourselves approached and sat on that sofa. The way we looked, we could've all been part of the same girlfriend crew or even related.

I leaned over and said, "Hi!"

One of the young women looked at me and said, "Hi! Are you in the business?"

I smiled and said, "No."

She grimaced, turned her whole body to the side,

put up "the hand," and ignored me, by engaging her friend in conversation, "Anyway! Blah, blah, blah, blah...."

My cousin and I looked at each other and shook our heads. When her actor friend entered the club, he found us. And, all night long and as if we were royalty, he graciously introduced us both (by name) to the entire cast of the movie and the who's who of Black Hollywood.

After her gracious friend, stepped away to bring us drinks, the young woman I had spoken to NOW humbly asked, "Y'all know them?"

Now, as if on cue, my cousin and I both said, "Yeah! Anyway...." And those words were punctuated by the very same body language she had given us earlier. Rolling neck, pursed lips, talk-to-the-hand gesture and all.

We never saw that actor or his friends again, except for on television, but for me, that moment was as priceless as a MasterCard.

Miracle on 42nd Street

I had just left the hair salon at around 11:15pm. Karen, my best friend and owner of Eternal Beauty, occasionally gave me a lift to the Gun Hill Road train station on her way home. I was hoping to be able to catch the M11 Express Bus down into Lower Manhattan. That would've left me closer to home and with minimal traffic, it would've been a quick, 45-minute trip. Unfortunately, I missed my bus by about 10 minutes.

Instead of waiting the half hour for another, I walked my beautified self across the street to catch the Flatbush bound #2 train down to 34th Street. That ride should've taken little more than an hour. But on this particular evening, the wait for that train was excruciatingly long.

When the train did arrive, the Subway car was half filled with young adults, looking like they were on their way to hang out on a Friday night. Girls, all had their hair and nails freshly done. Guys, with fresh haircuts, dressed in their best casual clothing. Everyone spread themselves out in the car, allowing themselves ample room and assuring they didn't invade anyone's personal space. The train itself, did the usual squealing and jerking, but crawled to 149th Street Grand Concourse.

When we pulled into 125th, a man that I assumed to be homeless entered and walked through, making an obnoxious pitch for passengers to fill his coffee cup with paper money. As he blew by me, I didn't notice any odor but would have assumed he had a foul odor by the looks of him. I know one thing, he was not satisfied with the fact that not a single coin donation dropped into his cup. So he planted himself smack in the middle of the Subway car instead of proceeding, and began to holler his random thoughts, "I'm from Maryland! I never been to a rodeo, and I like sandwiches with a lot of meat!"

New Yorkers can ignore anything. Despite his odd statements, no one so much as glanced in his direction. Those random assertions of his soon covered everything, from fragments of his life to bible verses. Competing against Beats and other stereo earbuds half the younger passengers were wearing, urged him to increase the volume on his storytelling. And he carried on spreading his message with spit flying from his mouth.

At 96th Street an Asian gentleman rushed in. He sat and looked across from him at the screaming man in the dingy cargo pants, upped and walked to the other end of the Subway car.

The train pulled into 72nd Street, a station that now had a crowded platform. Passengers piled in, quickly filling all the empty seats. Hands searched for space on poles.

The screamer went right back at it. "Maryland makes the best steaks! This ain't Maryland!"

The tourist that had just sat next to the screamer was a tall, beautiful, bright-skinned, black woman with big bushy hair. Her big, beautiful smile reminded me of my daughter. Young, she must've been in her early twenties. Her voice barreled with a pleasant accent when she screamed back, "Of course this isn't Maryland! I've been to Maryland!"

Now, of this trainload of passengers, those who had purposely been avoiding eye contact with this man were now engaged to see how he was going to react to her. I can only assume that like myself, they were quietly deciding how involved they'd get. The screamer's response was to ask, "Well, where you from?"

"I am from California!"

At that, he said, "California is a beautiful place!"

And she screamed back, "I know! That's why I live there!"

He cleared his throat and lowered his tone, "I also like Virginia. I've actually been all around the world."

"I've only been as far as West Coast to East Coast, and I've been down to the Caribbean twice. But I do like to travel."

He said, "I like to travel, too!" Now he screamed in excitement, but his voice turned somber when he added, "I just haven't been able to travel for a while."

At that, the tourist said, "Don't worry you'll get to travel again soon."

Now the rest of us, who have been there before, during, and after his entry into the car, we're all quietly laughing to ourselves.

But I noticed the Subway car had stopped somewhere between 72nd and 42nd Street and there was an announcement. *We are stalled. Due to a sick passenger, someone has pulled the Emergency Brake. We are stalled here until help arrives.*

We were stuck between the two stations for roughly forty-five minutes, confined to this one Subway car, but were actively eavesdropping on what had completely settled into pleasant comradery between this man and this young tourist. It was sheer beauty to witness this man's return to humanity, noticing how straight his posture became as he sat, his crossed legs, and how he he was so engrossed in their conversation that his smile became as big as hers. And by the time the train finally creeped into the Time Square Station, my cellphone read 1:30am. I saw no EMS workers in the station, but did see about 30 police officers.

The doors of the Subway car opened up and the homeless gentleman and the tourist step out through the foremost doors and smiled at each other. Just shy of giving him a hug, she said, "You have a great evening and be careful out here!"

He replied, "You too, and stay sweet, dear lady."

They walked off in different directions. Several police officers rushed in past them, looked up and down the Subway car, before exiting and boarding the next car over. Since someone had pulled the emergency brake, it seems they were now searching the whole train one car at a time. The tourist had walked down the platform. And I watched the strange gentleman's cargo pants casually exiting up the stairs, while these 30 or so police officers frantically searched in and about the Subway platform and cars for the missing "sick" passenger. Empty handed, they converged in the middle of the Subway platform, scratching their heads.

I was puzzled myself, trying to figure out which passenger in our car pulled the Emergency Brake. That man, turns out, may have just been going through a tough break. All he seemed to really need was someone to talk to him.

WITNESS

My best writing gal pal and I always spoke. Miriam would ask me, "What are you working on today?"

On Saturdays, my response was always the same, "Well, I've got this house to clean, the laundry to do, and if I finish early enough, maybe I'll scrub the floors, touch up the paintjob or start painting the bedroom. One of these days I'll hire myself a maid. Even if it's just for the day. I'll clean right alongside of her. I just need some help." The plan for Saturdays is always for me to do the cleaning in the morning and the writing in the afternoon, but by day's end, I'm always exhausted. I never seem to find even a sliver of creative time.

One Saturday, Miriam said to me, "You still cleaning that house? Girl, give yourself a break! That mess ain't going nowhere!" And she was right. My daughter had just turned twenty, three days earlier. She would've been my helping hands, but because she was away at college, housework for me had become a never-ending task. So I decided I was taking a break, even if I had to leave the laundry in a stinking heap. This Saturday, I was going to Freeport, Long Island to visit my Miriam. I was getting away from the routine in search of some much needed ME time. I was looking forward to this. This was going to be the day Miriam and I relaxed, sipped wine, and talked about writing, life, or nothing at all.

As soon as I purchased my ticket at Penn Station, I called her and let her know when the next train would be departing. Miriam mumbled a long list of instructions, something about riding the first car, an overpass, and some stairs. I said "yeah, okay" to everything because I didn't have a pen handy and I knew I would call her as soon as I reached her station anyway. I hung up, noticing on the digital sign overhead that the train had pulled into Track 14. I ran down, jumped onto the first car quite accidentally, because I had no clue which end of the train was which. On seeing an available empty seat, I sat and sat my big black purse down on the seat next to me.

Still out of breath, I made myself comfortable doing what I do best. I pulled out a book by Zora Neal Hurston and I went straight into creative mode. In my purse were two books that belonged to Miriam and a whole slew of books and things that fueled my muse. Zora, Jamaica Kincaid, Chris Abani, James Lee Burke, my writing journal, and notes. I was working on *Lipstick and Lingerie*. Fiction. It would be about a character that was thick and voluptuous, larger than life, sexually liberated, powerful, and overconfident, so different from me. What I had been writing, so far, had been dense in dialogue. My cheat tactic, because dialogue was always easiest for me. But I wanted to add texture to the new piece and give it depth. So much in life is said outside the scope of conversation. Actions are far more telling. And then, I wanted my character to be bold and sexually charged. In my opinion, erotica is cheesy, overdone, and cliché. Explicit ain't sexy. Most adults are already experts on the subject anyway. So why be graphic? We've all seen the parts. Do I really need to paint a picture for shock value? Too many details detract. This book would not be erotica, but I wanted it to be candid, with carefully chosen images. I would make my next project sexier by leaving certain things to the imagination. In my opinion, no one did that better than Zora. I rode most of the way on the LIRR, flipping through her collection of short stories, looking for logs floating along rivers, and bumble bees dripping with honey. I expected this to be just another long, uneventful, train ride.

I had been reading, so I barely noticed the train had emerged from the tunnel and was above ground. Still searching for inspiration, I pulled my nose out of my book long enough to look around the car. We writers are a strange breed. I admit being distracted by everything and I can find anything fascinating. I have always been accused of being absent minded. These absent minded moments feel like an out of body experience. I'm an observer in another realm, soaking up and analyzing everything I see, making mental notes. Once in a while when I'm in this dreamlike state, reality catches my attention and wakes me. This time it was the leg of a woman, extending out, blocking the aisle a few rows ahead of me. I noticed it was twitching.

I could tell this was a woman, because of the black leggings she wore and her stylish brown leather boots. I remember observing the jerky movement curiously. Still in my creative mindset, I remember thinking this was a nice, telling detail. The last time I had seen sharp jerky movements like that, it was a man seated across the room from me in a large, open cafeteria. He had been masturbating in public. I could only see the woman's leg, and at first I assumed she was masturbating too. But then, I noticed the top of the head of a toddler that was seated next to her. Maybe three years old, he was smiling, unalarmed. The woman's hand fell into view. At her side, it was empty and began jerking, like she was receiving shock treatments. Now, this seemed strange even to me, even for New York. Something told me to go check on her.

I sat my book down next to my purse, stood, and walked over to the woman. I touched her arm gently. "Ma'am," I said. "Are you okay?"

It was then that I saw her eyes roll up into the back of her head. At that moment, I was no longer a writer. This was no nice, telling detail. This was a human being. A person. She was having some kind of seizure or convulsions. She was a very petite woman who appeared to be Hispanic. She started sliding off the seat, so I held her, and screamed, "Help! Somebody get the conductor!"

Nobody moved, so I kept screaming the same thing over and over again, "Somebody get the conductor, please! This woman needs help!" But everyone seemed to be stunned. No one said anything. They just all stood and stared. All I knew about seizures was to put a spoon in the person's mouth, so that they wouldn't swallow their tongue and choke. I didn't have a spoon and I wasn't about to use my finger. I looked at the woman and her body collapsed, falling totally limp. All I could think was: *Lord, this woman is going to die in my arms and I don't know what to do.*

"Oh, God! Somebody please get the conductor," I screamed again. And when there was no response from anyone else, I did what came naturally...burst into tears. I cried and held this woman. I cried hysterically, like she was a member of my own family. Then, her baby began to cry. It was then that others on the train car sprang to action.

"It's okay, sweetheart. Mommy's okay," a woman with a soothing voice said.

"Lay her on the floor," someone else said. So, I did.

"Check her purse for a cell phone," another strange voice said. Another person grabbed her purse, found her cell phone, and began searching through it for the last numbers dialed.

Two conductors came rushing from either end. "Is there a doctor on this car? Any medical professional?"

"I'm a nurse!" A woman screamed, just before

74

rushing over. "She's unconscious!"

One of the conductors returned to the booth and soon we heard an announcement. If there is a doctor on this train, please come to the first car. *We have a medical emergency. We have a medical emergency.* They repeated the announcement several times. The train pulled into the next station and stayed there.

Two doctors rushed in and revived her somehow. "She regained consciousness," I heard one say.

The other said, "She'll be okay." But I saw she was still lying limp on the floor. I realized I was in the way, so I returned to my seat.

I then sent Miriam a text message. *Problem. Lady just had a seizure on my train. They stopped the train at Rockville Center.*

She texted me back. *Can u get off?*

I answered. *Yes.*

"I am on the phone with her boyfriend!" I heard a woman say. She asked him a series of questions, "She was on her way to meet you? Do you know if she has any medical condition? No? Can you come get her baby?"

Another woman was rubbing her baby's hand. I was glad for all of this, because by this point, I was so upset; I was a nervous wreck. I was no longer contributing, no longer able to think logically. Earlier, when I had asked the ailing woman if she was okay, the only response I was prepared for was a solid "yes." Under the circumstances, I didn't even have the foresight to check her purse, her pulse, pull the emergency break, or even to call 911, and I believe my cell phone might have been in my hand the whole time. I was no more help in the present situation than her child was. All my senses had left me and I was in shock. Ambulance workers rushed past with a stretcher. "How long has this woman been unconscious?" The whole train car looked at me.

"I don't know. I guess maybe eight minutes," I said.

The woman with a cell phone in her hand said, "I called 911 ten minutes ago, so it was more like twenty."

The woman seated right across from where the woman and her child were seated told them, "I didn't realize anything was wrong. I thought she was just playing with the baby."

My phone beeped. It was another text from Miriam. *On my way.*

Everyone else had the situation under control. The doctor said the woman would be okay. Now, that was enough. The paramedics were hooking her up to an IV. The woman with the cell phone was giving the EMS worker her boyfriend's cell phone number, so that he could pick up her son. I grabbed my bag and eased away, exiting through the back.

Once I made it down the stairs, I bawled. I cried because I was afraid and I didn't know what to do. I cried because I was ashamed of being that afraid in a crisis. I cried because I probably upset her baby. *What if she was an Epileptic and I was overreacting to what was just another seizure? I panicked and handled the situation all wrong.*

My mother is a powerful spirit, who always knows what to do in any and every given situation. She was a Verizon manager in the World Trade Center on 9/11. She made sure her whole staff evacuated, even when they were being assured by security that everything was under control. She even thought to check all the restrooms on her floor. She was a champion. Not me. There was chicken in this hero. And now fear had settled in my body tissue, giving me muscle spasms. I needed some comfort. I called my mother.

After I told her what happened, she said to me. "You may have just saved that woman's life. And do you realize where you are?"

I answered her, "Rockville Center."

"They're probably taking her to Mercy Hospital. You were there, too, twenty years ago."

I had forgotten. Twenty years prior, I was in a serious car accident when I was pregnant with my daughter. Unconscious, with head, neck, and back injuries, as well as multiple rib and pelvic fractures, I went into preterm labor on impact and was rushed by ambulance to Mercy Medical Center. I was in the critical care unit for a while. My daughter was born prematurely and we were both hospitalized for nearly a month.

My incident happened on the Southern State Parkway. One of the vehicles that struck the car I was in happened to be driven by an EMS worker, who just so happened to be one of the few who owned a cellular phone in 1991. We just so happened to be near Exit 15, two minutes away from Mercy Hospital. When I first sat in the car that night, I had forgotten to buckle up. I had only buckled my seatbelt minutes before. Seeing a van speeding towards our stalled vehicle, I did not expect to live through it. Long after, I wondered why I did. *Why am I still here? What is my purpose?*

Part of me felt that because I survived, what very easily could've been a tragic accident, this had to mean my purpose was to accomplish something monumental, to somehow save the world. My sexy fiction wasn't enough. Nothing I did seemed significant. For a very long time, I struggled with this. But in light of what happened on the LIRR, I realized something. I did not save that woman by myself. I did my part just by making others aware. And likewise, I didn't need to save the world singlehandedly. I didn't need to do everything or be everything for everyone. That's God's job. All I need to be is a link in the chain.

A Teachable Moment At Home

Onc morning my son, who was sixteen at the time, came to me. "Ma, I do not understand this poem and for homework I have to describe what it means."

I took a look at it and saw it was the famous one by Welsh poet Dylan Thomas, "Do Not Go Gentle into that Good Night." So I asked him, "What do you think it means?"

He said, "I don't know."

So I told him, "That poem was actually featured in the movie Dangerous Minds, starring Michelle Pfeiffer. They actually discuss the meaning of that poem in the movie."

He says, "Great! I'll look for it on Netflix!"

I said to him, "You can actually find that on YouTube. But before you do that, read the poem yourself three times and write down what YOU think it means. And then after that, you write down what the movie says. Be sure to let the teacher know that you saw that movie and in your essay, compare and contrast your thoughts against those points made in the movie and the reasons why you felt what you felt."

"Okay." He skips away and returns about fifteen minutes later with handwritten notes written all over his poem.

I asked, "Did you watch the movie?"

He said, "No."

Now I asked, "What do you think the poem is about?"

He said, "I think death, but that seems too easy."

I now say, "You are absolutely right! That poem is about death. You are a brilliant boy. Stop second guessing yourself. Sweetheart, sometimes the worst thing a person can do for you is to give you all the answers."

My Father's Jewelry Box

I remember one year, for argument's sake let's say it was Father's Day (but it may have actually been Christmas...I don't exactly recall. I was around 12 years old). But I remember my father had expensive taste and for this occasion, I wanted to get him something that he would buy for himself. I searched high and low until I saw a jewelry box, a wooden jewelry box with an antique car on top. That was it. I had to get this for my father.

I bought it and wrapped it and couldn't wait to see the expression on his face. To me, this was the perfect gift and I had already preselected the perfect spot for it, right atop his dresser. This jewelry box just so happened to be the perfectly matching grain of wood.

When I gave it to my father, he unwrapped it and said, "Oh wow! This is nice!"

I said, "You like it, for real?"

He said, "I love it!" But then he walked into the living room over to his bar that was chrome and had black smoked glass, and sat it on top.

Now upset, I said, "What did you do that for? It goes on the dresser! I bought it to match your dresser!"

He said, "It belongs on the bar."

I said, "No it doesn't! It's a jewelry box!"

My father always knew how to make room for his lesson, using his charm and humor. He opened the drawers, showing me they had no depth, but were embedded with cork disks. And then he said, "This is not a jewelry box! They're coasters!"

LYRICS

Eartha Watts Hicks

CHOCOLATE LOVE

This selection was first published in LOVE CHANGES the debut novel by Eartha Watts Hicks

You work so hard
Now, I know why
It's because you like
The finer things in life

It seems you have all
Life's luxuries
How is it you're missin'
What you need?

Chocolate Love every day
Can melt your fears away
And have you feeling new
That's what Chocolate can do

So many women
You like them fine
In different flavors
Like you like your wine

Consider yourself
A connoisseur?
Sometimes
Less is more

Chocolate love everyday
Can melt your fears away
And have you feeling...ooh
That's what Chocolate can do

GRAFFITI MURAL

Moet is okay
So is Dom Perignon
Caviar
And Filet Mignon
But really your lifestyle
Doesn't mean a thing
If you still feel incomplete.

GOOD FOR NOTHING SWEET TALKER

I think about you
And I die of curiosity.
I've come too far to
Turn around;
You're distracting me.
And now I have to
Satisfy my curiosity.
I have to ask you.
How did you get so smooth?

I could close my eyes
In the dead of night
And come to life the moment, I receive your call.
Your words as sweet as wine.
I'm drunk on every line.
Tell me anything and I believe it all.

But I'm no fool.
Back to reality
What I want from you.
Is more than what you want from me.
Here is all my love.
When you only want a piece.
And I know that
I'm worth more, so much more.

Good for nothing
Sweet talker.

GRAFFITI MURAL

I fear and I feel you.
So, irresistibly
Tempting.
Please tell me
How did you get so smooth?

I NEVER SAID I WAS YOUR MAN

This selection was first published in the July 2014 issue of Urban Image Magazine.

You and me were only having fun.
Girl, you knew that was the way it was supposed
to be.
Then you decided fun wasn't enough.
That it was love for you, when it wasn't love for
me

I never tried to lead you on.
I didn't do anything wrong.
You were the one who fell for me.
If someone's to blame, girl, it isn't me.

You say that you gave me your all.
Crying, how I did you wrong.
But girl, don't you understand
I never said I was your man.

You wanted more than I could give,
And you felt more than I did.
It's not my fault you're feeling bad.
I never said I was your man.

The sex was good.
But in your mind
You thought you were making love to me.
I never lied or said you were the one.
Now, I wonder just what did you expect from me.

Did you think you'd get what you want?

GRAFFITI MURAL

Did you think I would grow to love you?
It takes two, no matter what you think.
Think what you want, but don't you blame me.

You thought what you wanted to think.
I never promised anything.
Do you understand?

Now that you're hurt,
You wanna put it all on me.
You took that chance.
What did you expect?
I never said I was your man.

POETRY

GRAFFITI MURAL

WE SHARE OUR WORLD FOR A REASON

We all should be proud of
who we are,
where we're from
and respect everyone's
individual right to be just as proud.

We could all love ourselves enough
and appreciate differences,
differences in background, class, culture.

We would all understand being Pro-Me
does not require anyone to be Anti-You,
Or live with US against THEM divisiveness.

But for the stubborn and pigheaded few,
fools who refuse to see shifts in society,
radical divides melding indistinguishably,
thanks to biological, extended, spiritual family
in a continuum.

Someday, minority and majority
will not be defined by race,
but redefined by attitude
and understanding....

Hate anywhere hurts everyone.

Eartha Watts Hicks

ONE SALTY SEASON

A seasoned woman lying on the beach...
She's no longer just musing,
Staring at crystal clear waves
As they beat against the shore.

She's seeing out into murky waters,
Into the middle of the ocean,
Into the depths and disturbances of raging
storms,
Wondering.

Who will be in the same boat?
Who will bail?
Who will be in tow?
Who will be rocking this boat?
Who will be helping to row?

GRAFFITI MURAL

I SAW AN AFRICAN QUEEN

Mozambique Sapphire,
Gemstone fit for a crown,
Mystique ever so luminous.

I saw an African Queen.
Wrapped in iridescent, jewel-toned silks,
An actual queen from Africa
With skin black
As a night without stars,
Carrying a purse worth...
More than my home.

Eartha Watts Hicks

GOOD MUSE SINGS

Each day,
My muse hums before break,
Before street percussionists scratch and pound
To traffic's screechy backbeat.
Before chirping pigeons cry
High G,
Before a lone perpetual flame peeks,
Sneaks in chasing red,
Hitchhikes a band across horizon,
Leaves all feeling the blues,
My muse's verse
Has long since crossed...
A bridge
Solo
A cappella
In bass tenor
Scatting a crescendo
Vibrato,
Altro
And then again,
He hums.

A POET WHO LOSES A NOTE
(Limerick)

I wrote an incredible poem...
But I misplaced it.
In my search for lost poem,
I stumble across ten more
I don't remember writing.
I know they're mine.
My handwriting.
I guess I'm scribbling on the go—
Words,
Letters,
Seeds.
On the bus or Subway,
On the run,
Crafted everywhere,
Standing in line,
Within any sliver of idle time,
Without realizing,
I dump thoughts.
I craft poems.
Though, I *still* have to yet to find
The poem with best timeless one-line,
The other nine I did find are....
Better.

So, I'll keep searching.
That's a no-brainer.

WRITERS BLEED

Ink pens leak blood red pain
Into perpetual threads of truth called story.
Express the unfathomable
In bite-sized morsels.
Digestible,
Though only eventually understood.

Eluding until that eventual epiphany:

The smart know everything.
The wise know nothing.
Fools school the smart.
Fools went to college.
Prayer offers the only true solace.
Together we form solutions.
Body of Christ,
We are knowledge.

GRAFFITI MURAL

INTERRACIAL DATING

Interracial dating?
I straddle the fence
Of appreciation for other races
And sheer pride and preference
for my own.

I respect that others love us,
Because we are loveable,
But wonder:
How can we remember
WE are QUEENS,
If our KINGS don't choose us?
Or abuse us.

Do we lack the self-esteem
to truly love each other?

If we do not love ourselves,
Why can't other clans love us?

Eartha Watts Hicks

BEAUTIFUL PEOPLE

We stand out,
Overdo,
Emboss our stamp on simple,
Reimagine,
Reinvent,
Invigorate.
Look now!
It's unrecognizable.

We refuse to be outdone.
With genius encrypted genetics,
We expose mediocrity,
Surpass the incredible,
Shock.

Our efforts built this entire world,
Shake it,
Make it crane its neck,
Mock,
But ultimately mimic our best,
Even in the absence of respect.

    Side Note:
    Some stargazers pretend
    They don't see Venus.
    That's okay, honey,
    They can watch Uranus!

Only when thoroughly impressed
Would the compliments, "Nice,""Tight,""Sick,"
"Slick" ever slip past lips
Of those with thick skin the color of crude oil.

GRAFFITI MURAL

We are boldly critical.
Blame the beauty of our try.
Ascribe the might of our Maker.
But don't deny.

EVERY BREATH IS A PRAYER

Every breath is a prayer.
Every untainted thought I think,
Every sight I behold,
Every instance I stand,
Every single step I press
I owe Him.

SHARING KOOL-AID WITH MY ROAD DOG

Left hand partially numb
Post-carpal tunnel release,
I pour myself a drink,
Filling my glass past its brim,
Spilling, Kool-Aid into Kitty's food bowl.
Dry rainbow kibble that had been ignored half the
day,
He now gobbles like fried catfish.
Red Kool-Aid soaked, it's a new delicacy for Kitty.
Makes me wonder...
What if my cat,
Better yet my road-dawg,
Needed to undergo another kidney stone surgery.
"1-800-KAT-CARE. How may I direct your call?"
"Okay. I need to know. What's my current line of
credit?"

EVER-FORGIVING

Good intentions abate to waste
For those with ill-intended interests.

Aching hearts always state,
"I'll never bother again."

NEVER has no integrity,
NEVER is never long enough.

NEVER is always fast arriving
For the ever-forgiving.

BLEW STREAK

I blew a streak,
Almost.
Blue-streaks
Enlighten,
Whistle inspiration
Repeated in whispers.
Flashes of imagination
Surge
True artistry
To felt tip.

SUN'S SCREAMING

Sun's screaming,
Streaming a blue water-colored high
And daydreams.
My poetry flows.

Didn't you know I'm a poet?
Since a girl yay-high!
Now, ask how do I do
A haiku in 5-7-5...
    How high is the sky?
    When you look up at the sun,
    Don't you wanna fly?

YOUR OWN WAY

Pick your passion.
Stick needles in sick kids.
Massage spices into lamb.
Make music bubble up and burst.
GO satisfy your Jones,
Bruise your body and your ego.
Play games, kick game or shoot game.
The choice is yours.
Scream your secrets!
Be your dream.
Drown your misery in chlorine.
Write. Or read.
Or write to read until split infinitives and
dangling participles leave you hanging,
Breathless.
Then, come back from that.
Take a nap.
Wake up to make up.
Beat your face.
Punch a bag or fix cars.
Race, skate, fly, paint the town.
Paint the clouds and some happy trees.
Plant a tree.
Watch the stars.
Name a star 'Bea.'
Positively, switch your new do to one you
wouldn't usually do.
Whatever it takes to ensure your Jones is
completely satisfied.
Do you all the way.
Just keep doing you...your own way.

SHOCK-FREE REALITY

I am remembering
When 35 was old.
No one became seriously ill.
The aging simply fell asleep,
Never again to wake from their dreams.

I am remembering
When a child would stay in a child's place,
Out of grown folks faces, mouths, conversations,
Would be seen, not heard
Or go outside and play.

Now an adult,
I face harsh realities,
Realizing that I was busy, being distracted;
Way too distracted
By fairytales, fables, myths,
Failing to notice
That life itself was always surreal.

Eartha Watts Hicks

SUMMERS DOWN SOUTH

My childhood summers spent Down South
Taught me appreciation.
A lesson
The moment I stepped my polished shoes
Onto my family's red dirt acre.
Ghetto red bricks now appealed like castle stone.
By day, I'd race in white "tennis shoes."
My dust cloud, a short leg behind my barefoot
cousin's.
Board games? Bored games.
Can't Easy-Bake mud pies, but they'll just have
to do.
We'd never bring sunscreen; I'm easily baked by
noon.
Quenching my thirst at the water pump,
I'd kill for an ice cube.
By nightfall, call me the mosquito feeder
And avid reader; there's only Channel 2.
Early rest on the makeshift bed
Rags that feel like nails
Till I rise at the rooster's crow
Walk the eerie walk in the dim of Dawn.
Out to the outhouse
Where I handle my private business
In the company of busy, buzzing flies.
The long journey back,
I am anticipating my room, my toys, color TV!
Home to the projects to watch the Brady's
And play with Barbie.
No Dreamhouse.
Still I am happy...just to be me.

BOUQUET OF FLORA

Dear Flora, dear Flora,
Perfect Rose share bouquets;

Daisy ne'er dare bully Lily
Neither deem Violet inferior,
Shan't complain,
"Thy Baby's Breath,
We cast thee flawed and mediocre!"

For the array,
Blends as spray.

Mums the word,
As each share the language of Blossom's smile.
Incessantly and
In one accord,
All
Suffer each other to bloom.

THICK LIPS

Thick lips, soft.
Thick lips, moist.
Thick lips, no one appreciates at 9 years old.
Juvenile insults, make 'em wanna hide.

At 17,
Thick lips reasons so fine.

Word on the streets, thick lips fire.
Thick lips frame pretty teeth, sexy smile,
Form unseen obscenities.

When Vogue vague
EnVogue fully confirmed.
Thick lips press promises.
Whisper profanities,

Tease to please
Apply thick lips to thick lips.
A foretaste of sweet.

GRAFFITI MURAL

IT TAKES A LICKING

Why lick my ear with promises
When I straddle your lap;
Fill my womb with your spilled seed,
Fill my heart with sap?

Sap's a spring
When things are sweet.
Sap's hot and ever flowing.

Sap gets hard
When things turn cold.
That's how hearts get broken.

Eartha Watts Hicks

OUR SYNERGY – ABSTRACT EROTICA

You were created for me to discover...
What would someday help me uncover
Who I need to be.

You are you,
I am me....

Our synergy isn't symmetrical.
Our chemistry's beyond sexual.
Complimentary rather than compatible
With deference for differences....

You are enough,
Sum, substance,
My catalyst,
While I serve as your base,
A safe, neutral place to restore.

You are you,
I am me,
Together, we can be...more.
Together, we can be
Everything we were meant to be.

RELEASE ENDORPHINS

Release endorphins.
Babyface.
Stuff with truffles.
Moscato Marinated,
Syrupy manipulations become truth.

Next Kemistry.
Transformative,
As you pour your real self into
And sip from
The chalice.

That would grow wood
And can...
Turn Pinocchio into a real boy...
Into a better man.

UNDERSTANDING THE COUPLES FORMULA

How could something be better than nothing at all,
When not enough would never sustain?
No one human is everything
Bound up in one.
But must it be 80/20?
Why not YOU and ME; US both, each as 50% of WE?
And let our respective 50% expound exponentially...
Because we each keep it 100.
100% + 100% should equal 200%.
Coupling should double, like the numbers suggest.
Like 1 and 1 equals 2,
$E = MC^2$
And πr^2 brings us full circle.
Relative to Einstein I'm no real genius,
But the way I see it,
Let everything double!

GRAFFITI MURAL

BE MY

Be my...
First call early morning,
Last call of the day,
Unnecessary apologies,
Unlimited promise,
Power to forward and still time
Transform wonder into gratitude....

Will you be mine?

Eartha Watts Hicks

LA-SHAWN @ DAWN

A lovely new day breaks.
What's mine is mine.
And he do
What dew does.
He makes
My bronze face blush.
Flush.
I'm flustered in a good way.

Welcoming
Everyone who'll see me,
Screaming "Hello, Sunshine!'

I won't say jack back,
But I'll be beaming.

Lit from inside,
I'll brandish
A mile-wide smile.

And while my eyes may hint of why,
May faintly reveal quality time spent,
These guilty, wine-stained lips of mine'll seal.
Concealing words on the tip of my tongue,
"He's Heaven sent."

GRAFFITI MURAL

#GROWINGUPWITHMYNAME

My great-aunt's mother
Was a midwife in rural South Carolina,
Birthing 18 of her own,
With only three surviving.

I'm another Eartha.
It's my great-aunt's name.
She was last born.
I was first born.
Family and friends refer to namesake by
nickname.
#GrowingUpWithMyName

The 70s.
When I'm not Eartha, Wind & Fire,
I'm Eartha Butt Boogie,
But I can dig it!
#GrowingUpWithMyName

A colorful educator
Could've slayed
As a stand-up comic.
"'Watts' your name?'"
#GrowingUpWithMyName

Another punny.
"Eartha Watts!
No wonder you're so bright
And get great grades in Science!"
#GrowingUpWithMyName

Later learning 'Eartha' was
Historical choice of
Deep South midwives.
Gave endangered, black baby girls
'Staying power!"
#GrowingUpWithMyName

My whole life long,
Always hearing, "Eartha?
Any relation to Eartha Kitt?"
But never once replying...
"Why ask me that?
My last name ain't Kitt!"
#GrowingUpWithMyName

GRAFFITI MURAL

A DEFINITION OF SELFIE

I am...
Three dimensional,
Layered,
Complex
Flawed.

To experience
The full embodiment of me...
Is to get more than what you see
In a one-inch square.

Eartha Watts Hicks

MIGHTY WRITING

I can
Map ideas
From inception to my ideals,
Change the past,
Orchestrate the future,
Detract, propel,
Correct current affairs and bad situations
Employing just my imagination.

I can
Conceptualize,
Allure and entice,
Sacrifice or highlight;
List tips to solve issues,
A plethora of possibilities.
Point out a penchant
To progress peers.
Stroke my panache
That in my own little world,
My own stroke can swirl
The imagination of many.

I caress the instrument in my right hand,
Cast sky and wind to canvas,
Because it is my right to right wrongs
And replenish the strong
With fresh lyrics,
When old songs...stop working.

YOU SHOULD GIVE YOUR BOOKS AWAY
FOR FREE...ALL THE TIME!

True.
But then, who's gonna pay my bills?
Can me and my 9 kids pack up, pick up,
Come live in with you?
Could you buy my paper, too?
I'm running low.
I just checked my stash.
Nowadays, reams of paper cost wads of cash.
And about those nine kids, I really only got 2.
We likes to eat king crab legs with drawn butter,
And they got good appetites, too!
You can pay ALL my bills if you wanna.
That's really up to you.
Or you can buy my book.
I'll pay my own bills myself,
And only eat tuna when and if I really want to.

Eartha Watts Hicks

#BROKEISNOJOKE

We're living in a time
When a dollar's worth a dime,
And folks lack common sense...

Cause we're all in a pickle,
Needing just another nickel
To make a dollar out of 15¢.

#BrokeIsNoJoke

BONUS

Writing My Uveitis Experience

Many of us are battling a health issue, struggling through treatment, hoping for a cure, reaching for a plateau where our condition is in remission or, at the very least, is under control. Those of us who are know: battling an ailment can be taxing, not only physically, but emotionally.

In December of 2005, I awoke in the middle of one evening and everything was black. Even after I allowed my eyes to adjust to dim lighting, all I saw were shapes outlined in florescent colors—pinks, yellows, greens, and blues. I didn't panic. I assumed that I was overtired and went back to sleep. The next morning I could see again, but once I looked in the mirror, I noticed the whites of my eyes were red. Assuming this was conjunctivitis, I scheduled an appointment with my physician, especially since around this same time, I was walking around with this random pain in my side. When I made it to my doctor visit, my main concern was this pain I was experiencing in the kidney area. My doctor scheduled me for a CAT scan but was more concerned with my eyes. Once he examined them, he did not prescribe the drops for pink eye as I expected. He immediately referred me to an eye specialist. The eye specialist then referred me to another specialist. The condition I was ultimately diagnosed with is called bilateral

Uveitis.

According to medlineplus.com, Uveitis is an inflammation that occurs inside the eye, affecting the uvea. Or as my Uveitis specialist explained to me, my white blood cells were attacking the insides of both my eyes, causing damage to my own eye tissue. This rare condition is not contagious but can be caused by a number of factors, among them, parasitic infection and Sarcoidosis. My CAT scan results revealed various complications throughout my lungs, kidneys, liver, and gallbladder, all benign tumors. Receiving these results, my Uveitis specialist immediately pinpointed Sarcoid as the cause, because from his experience that was the one condition likely to affect the eyes, liver, and other organs. He recommended that I get a chest x-ray. But, by this point I was fed up with bad news at doctor's appointments, so I put that off, delaying farther and farther, until ultimately, my own primary care physician scheduled the chest x-ray. Sure enough, I was diagnosed with Stage I Sarcoid. The Sarcoid, for the most part was asymptomatic. Dealing with Uveitis was another matter all together.

Initially, upon being diagnosed with bilateral Uveitis, I was only mildly concerned. My doctor prescribed some steroid drops, and I began treatment, prayerfully optimistic. In my mind, Uveitis was as easily treated and cured as pinkeye. Considering them one and the same, I was sure after a few drops and a few short weeks, this "problem" would be taken care of, and everything would return to normal. But then, somewhere around my second or third visit to my specialist, I encountered a fellow Uveitis patient in the waiting room, a woman who had been battling this for eight years. I talked to this woman and listened, as she gave me her account of cortisone eye injections with a very long needle, subsequent cataract diagnosis, glaucoma, eye surgery, and vision loss. I immediately became depressed.

After that, though the changes in my vision were gradual, for a while, my experience chronicled exactly what that other patient described. First, I saw tiny dark spots. These later expanded until they gave me the impression that a swarm of large bugs were flying at me. In Uveitis terms, these are known as "floaters." Then, in addition to this, my vision occluded with dark threads, first one, and then others, until it seemed as if I were viewing the world through a filthy screen. In Uveitis terms, this is known as "spider webs." Uveitis is a condition where white blood cells attack eye tissue, as if they were a foreign body or implanted, or simply did not belong as part of one's body system. This being the case, my vision was going through some changes. My eyes became extremely sensitive to light. I adapted by doing everything in the dark and wearing dark shades in the sunlight. For months at a time, no one around me could turn on bright lights, as that would cause me more eye pain, and the pain was intense, burning the equivalent of trying to recover from exposure to chlorine or sand, with one difference. The pain was constant. My night vision diminished, I could no longer see beyond a few feet. Because this problem was occurring within the eyes, the changes in my vision could not be improved with corrective lenses. My doctor changed my prescription, from the Predforte drops to Cellcept, an immunosuppressant. I was in agony, but I did experience a brief reprieve. I was given a software program known as EyeQ that was actually intended to teach speed reading. Somehow, this program strengthened my eye muscles, and with the medication improved my vision. My Uveitis was controlled, and I was relieved. My vision seemed to be returning to normal.

But then, for some reason unbeknownst to me, my health insurance provider refused to honor my prescription, refusing because it was not a generic drug. At the time, Cellcept was not available in any generic form and was also extremely expensive. While costing nearly $100 a pill, one pill daily was required for my condition. My doctor was now required to send in medical evidence proving that, for my condition, Cellcept was "medically necessary." Thank God this young doctor was relentless about that. For the next two and a half weeks, this doctor, the pharmacy, and insurance company faxed paperwork back and forth and played phone tag. The matter was soon resolved after about three or four weeks, but my vision deteriorated. According to my doctor, I experienced a fifty percent loss of vision. At one point, I was unable to read. My expression contorted to the point where I always appeared angry, but it was actually me wincing from the pain and squinting, to help me see clearer. My doctor now had me on both Cellcept and the Predforte drops. And soon, the skin at outside corners of my eyes bore light circles where my eye drops had drained and bleached away pigment from my skin. I now wore sunglasses during the day and evening, even in the wintertime. Soon, I was also diagnosed with cataracts.

Meanwhile, I was still writing but now had a renewed appreciation for everything I saw. Beauty was in dust, in clouds, in any and everything, and that love was transferred to the page when I wrote anything descriptive. For the most part, though, I otherwise remained quiet during all this. My family knew, but I didn't even share what I was going through with some of closest friends. Yet, I found myself preparing for the worst, instructing those who depended on me how to carry on in my absence. Even though I was praying for healing, it was as if instead of counting my blessings, part of me was actually counting down, and I was only allotted eight years. I put on weight, partly because of the steroid medication I was taking, but mainly due to the fact that I sought comfort in Häagen-Dazs chocolate chip cookie dough.

In the midst of this, my mother reminded me, "If you pray don't worry; if you worry don't pray." At some point, I don't remember when exactly, but the message sank in. I realized I had to make up my mind to either live in fear or live by faith. I had to stop believing what my own eyes were telling me and trust God. And even though this was a dark time in my life in more ways than one, I buckled down and focused on the positives. I had children to care for and the love and support of family and friends. God had brought me through so many trials in the past,

GRAFFITI MURAL

"No weapons formed against me shall prosper!" Surely, He wouldn't leave me now. "All power is of God Creator of Heaven and Earth."

Then, at the insistence of my neighbor, I reached out. I asked a pastor we knew to pray for me. When he did, he told me at my next doctor's visit, my doctor wouldn't find anything wrong. Sure enough, my next visit, my doctor saw no trace of the cataracts, no sign of inflammation, and he remarked how my eyes "never looked better." God heals.

Today, thank God, my Uveitis is controlled. My vision is great. But as a result of the experience, I can relate to those who are battling. Health battles are not just physical; they are also of the spirit. Depression does nothing but impede progress. If we expect the worst, more than likely we will not be disappointed. Instead, we should educate ourselves, with our objective being health and healing, disregard the gory stories, and focus on the positives. Although, we may be suffering, we must nevertheless, stay focused, follow through with treatment responsibly, and above all remain faithful. Even when we are faced with "facts," we need to trust God. Because, after all, the battle isn't ours; it's His.

ABOUT THE AUTHOR

Eartha Watts-Hicks is a writing fellow of the Center for Black Literature's North Country Institute and a member of the acclaimed Harlem Writers Guild. She the former director of publications for Cultivating Our Sisterhood International Association, a 501(c)(3) and now serves editor-in-chief for Harlem World's Magazine. In June of 2013, Eartha received the Just R.E.A.D. Award in fiction from the NYCHA branch of the NAACP and was named their literacy ambassador. Eartha Watts Hicks is now editor-in-chief of Harlem World Magazine and CEO of Earthatone Books.

Other titles available from Earthatone Books....

Weaver by Miriam Kelly Ferguson
(ISBN 13: 9780991489206)

Love Changes by Eartha Watts Hicks
(ISBN 13: 9780991489213)

Made in the USA
Middletown, DE
29 March 2017